SERIES EDITOR: TONY

OSPREY AIRCRAFT OF T

Austro Hungarian Aces
of World War 1

Christopher Chant

OSPREY
PUBLISHING

Front cover
In July 1918 Frank Linke-Crawford flying a Phönix D.I of *Flik 60J* fought an inconclusive battle with a Sopwith Camel on the southern edge of the Dolomite range over Feltre. Both aircraft sustained considerable battle damage but neither was shot down.
(cover artwork by Keith Woodcock)

Title spread
Von Banfield is seen in the cockpit of a Lohner Type S (modified Type E) flying boat after an unsuccessful sortie against French raiders on 14 March 1916. In the 'sS.3' designation on the hull of the 'boat, the 's' stands for Stahlhertz (rotary engine) and the 'S' for Schule (school). Other lower case prefixes were 'b' and 'm' indicating the use of Benz and Mercedes engines respectively

First published in Great Britain in 2001 by Osprey Publishing
Elms Court, Chapel Way, Botley, Oxford, OX2 9LP

ISBN 1 84176 376 4

Page design by TT Designs, T & B Truscott
Cover Artwork by Keith Woodcock
Aircraft Profiles by Mark Rolfe and Harry Dempsey

Origination by Grasmere Digital Imaging, Leeds, UK
Printed in Hong Kong through Bookbuilders

02 03 04 05 06   10 9 8 7 6 5 4 3 2 1

AUTHOR'S NOTE
The author would like to express his deep appreciation for the assistance provided in writing this book by the pioneering work of Dr Martin O'Connor.

For a catalogue of all Osprey Publishing titles please contact us at:

Osprey Direct UK,
PO Box 140,
Wellingborough,
Northants NN8 4ZA, UK
E-mail: **info@ospreydirect.co.uk**

Osprey Direct USA,
c/o Motorbooks International,
729 Prospect Ave,
PO Box 1,
Osceola, WI 54020, USA
E-mail: **info@ospreydirectusa.com**

Or visit our website: **www.ospreypublishing.com**

Austro-Hungarian Aces
of World War 1

CONTENTS

AN EMPIRE ABOUT TO COLLAPSE

I n 1914 the Austro-Hungarian Empire was still considered one of the 'Great Powers', but was in reality nothing of the sort. The single most important player in the politics and economics of central Europe for 300 years until the end of the Napoleonic Wars in 1815, Austria-Hungary had then failed significantly to keep up with the pace of modernisation, both political and economic, set by the countries of western Europe.

This multi-ethnic Empire was ruled from Vienna by men of Austrian origin who were woefully ignorant of the mass of nationalist aspirations that were about to tear the Empire apart. The economy of Austria-Hungary was still largely agrarian, and her armed forces were fragmented by the overall unwillingness of conscripts, mostly from non-German speaking regions, to serve an Empire that did not recognise their aspirations and placed over them officers of whom some 75 per cent spoke only German, the language of the ruling class. It is one of history's great ironies that World War 1 (1914–1918), the conflict that ended with the total collapse of the Austro-Hungarian Empire, was sparked by Austria-Hungary herself.

Just before the outbreak of World War 1, the balance of power in Europe was maintained by two major diplomatic and military groupings, the Triple Alliance and the Triple Entente. The Triple Alliance comprised Austria-Hungary, Germany and Italy, and the Triple Entente was formed by France, Russia and the United Kingdom. At this time the Austro-Hungarian Empire's primary concern was the situation on its southern frontier, where the ever-volatile northern Balkans seethed with problems. In this region Serbia and Romania had secured their independence from the Ottoman Empire in 1878, the year in which the Austro-Hungarian Empire assumed the administration of Bosnia-Herzegovina, which she annexed in 1908. Farther to the south and east, Bulgaria gained her independence from the Ottoman Empire in 1908. As a result of the two Balkan Wars (1912–1913) Bulgaria, Greece and Serbia further increased their territories at the expense of the Ottoman Empire, and Albania emerged as an independent country to the east and south of the kingdom of Montenegro, bounded on its northern side by Bosnia-Herzegovina.

The Emperor Karl I inspects some of his men at Kezdi-Vasarhely in Romania during 1917. The taller of the two men facing the emperor is Otto Jindra, the Bohemian-born commander of *Flik 1*

Like Serbia, Russia had ambitions in the Balkans and therefore opposed the Austro-Hungarian annexation of Bosnia-Herzegovina. However, German support for Austria-Hungary negated Russian opposition, but left the neighbouring Serbs in a turmoil of thwarted nationalist ambition. On 28 June 1914, the heir to the Austro-Hungarian throne, the Erzherzog (Archduke) Franz Ferdinand, visited Sarajevo, the capital of Bosnia-Herzegovina. He and his wife were assassinated by a Serb nationalist fanatic. This event triggered the outbreak of World War 1. On 23 July Austria-Hungary delivered an ultimatum to Serbia, which conceded only in part. Serbia mobilised on 25 July, and three days later Austria-Hungary declared war. Russia mobilised against Austria-Hungary, which triggered the German declaration of war against Russia on 1 August and, in accordance with the long-established strategic Schlieffen Plan, against France on 3 August. Germany made her first offensive moves not against Russia but against France via neutral Belgium and Luxembourg, which caused Britain to declare war on Germany on 4 August as Britain was a guarantor of Belgian neutrality.

The initial line-up of World War 1's protagonists was completed on 6 August, when Austria-Hungary declared war on Russia. Of the six members of the Triple Entente and Triple Alliance, only Italy at this stage opted for a cautious neutrality, declaring that Austria-Hungary had made void the requirements of the Triple Alliance by her declarations of war.

The members of the Triple Entente became known as the Allied Powers, while those of the now Double Alliance were generally known as the Central Powers. Later European adherents to the Allied Powers were Italy, Portugal, Romania and Greece, while the Ottoman Empire and Bulgaria joined the Central Powers. Japan and the USA joined the Allied Powers in 1914 and 1917 respectively.

Under General Franz Conrad von Hotzendorf, its chief-of-staff, the Austro-Hungarian army had prepared two offensive plans. Plan B was to be implemented for a campaign against Serbia alone, while Plan R was to be used in the event of hostilities against Russia as well as Serbia. Conrad initially deployed his forces for Plan B but changed his mind in favour of Plan R after the Austro-Hungarian deployment had started. Austro-Hungarian forces were eventually committed on four major fronts – against the Italians on a western Italian front, the Serbs on a southern Serb front, the Allies on a still more southern Macedonian front, and the Russians on the Eastern Front. Austria-Hungary lacked the reserves and the combination of economic and industrial strength to support the army in a protracted war, and was compelled to call increasingly on Germany for both manpower and weapons support.

The war was a total disaster for Austria-Hungary which, with Turkey, lost more territory than Germany. On 3 November 1918 Austria-Hungary secured an armistice from the Allied powers with effect from the following day, ending Austria-Hungary's war a week before that of Germany. The result was the dissolution of the Austro-Hungarian Empire. Austria and Hungary became separate nations, losing territory to the new kingdom of Yugoslavia, the new state of Poland, and to Italy and Romania. Other parts of the erstwhile Austro-Hungarian Empire became independent as the new state of Czechoslovakia.

THE AUSTRO-HUNGARIAN AIR ARMS

Despite its creation in 1893 of a balloon corps for artillery spotting and battlefield reconnaissance, in the early days of powered flight the Austro-Hungarian military had little interest in aviation, being happy with the purchase of a few examples of the Etrich Taube (dove) wire-braced monoplane created by the Austrian designer Igo Etrich. By 1912, however, the progress made by a number of other European nations in the creation of primitive air arms prompted the Austro-Hungarians to create a committee to investigate military aeronautics. The committee reported that an air arm was required, and as a result an officer named Emil Uzelac was promoted to Oberst (colonel) and tasked with the creation of what later became the *kaiserliche und königliche Luftfahrtruppen* (imperial and royal aviation troops). This was generally abbreviated to kuk LFT or just LFT, the prefix indicating that the nation's ruler, Franz Josef, was Emperor of Austria and King of Hungary.

At the time aged 44, Uzelac was a rounded man with a spectrum of talents that included horsemanship, fencing, skiing and possession of a master mariner's certificate. Although he had no experience at all of flying, Uzelac quickly remedied this defect and within only a few months was regarded as one of the best pilots in Austria-Hungary. Until the end of the Austro-Hungarian Empire's existence, Uzelac was the real chief of the LFT, and in this difficult task he fought hard against Austria-Hungary's lack of modern industries and misappreciation of the demands of modern war struggling to overcome the shortages of equipment with which his

The commander of the Austro-Hungarian army air service throughout World War 1 was Oberst (later Generalmajor) Emil Uzelac, seen here in conversation with the men of a unit flying the Hansa-Brandenburg CI two-seater *(Bruce Robertson)*

Among the earliest aircraft acquired by the fledgling air arm of the Austro-Hungarian army air service was the Etrich Taube monoplane, officially known as the Type A class *(Bruce Robertson)*

units had to contend. The quality of Uzelac as a man and commander was shown by the fact that in addition to his tasks as an administrator and trainer, he was a frequent test pilot of aircraft for the LFT.

On the outbreak of Austria-Hungary's war with Russia, Serbia and Montenegro, the LFT's total strength was 39 heavier-than-air craft, one dirigible airship and 10 balloons. The heavier-than-air craft were of the Etrich Taube monoplane type, in variants known to the LFT as the A I and A II, and the Lohner Pfeil (arrow) biplane type. These aircraft were operated by just 85 pilots deployed in nine *Fliegerkompanien* (flying companies). Russia and her allies had no real strength in the air, but for operations in Galicia and the Balkans there was very clearly an urgent need for more aircraft, especially after the value of the aeroplane for tactical reconnaissance came to be appreciated. Austro-Hungarian resources were inadequate to remedy this deficiency, and the Austro-Hungarians approached the Germans with the sort of plea that was soon to become all too common in Austria-Hungary's war effort. Germany had few aircraft to spare, but grudgingly supplied some Aviatik and Rumpler B-category unarmed biplanes.

This bought time for Austria-Hungary to begin the creation of the new factories that would be needed for the production of airframes and engines for the LFT. Industrialisation had come late to Austria-Hungary (her steel output in 1914 was only two million tons by comparison with Germany's 17 million tons and four, four and nine million tons respectively for

In 1915 the Austro-Hungarians captured this Albatros B I from the Russians, who had themselves seized the machine at an earlier date *(Bruce Robertson)*

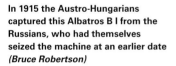

France, Russia and the UK). Facilities were limited. It was immediately apparent that few existing firms could handle orders for more than 50 airframes, and then on the basis of hand manufacture rather than any 'production line' basis. The only significant airframe manufacturer was Lohner, although the government had a small aircraft-manufacturing facility at Fischamend. The availability of useful aero engines was better, however. Daimler and Warschalowski, and Eissler & Company (known as Hiero), were able to supply a series of water-cooled inline engines of ever increasing capability, and there was also an extensive network of subcontractors working on engines. Air-cooled rotary engines, offering a higher power/weight ratio (important in the aircraft types typical of the period from 1914 to 1916), could not be produced, however, because Austria-Hungary had a shortage of castor oil, which was essential for the lubrication of such engines.

Italy's declaration of war on 15 May 1915 opened another front and imposed a still greater strain on the resources of the LFT. This was exacerbated by the fact that operations over the Italian Front were more dangerous than those over the Eastern Front as a result of the mountainous terrain. An engine failure over the Alps almost always resulted in the death of the pilot in the resultant crash landing. In the short term the LFT was fortunate that the Italian air arm was in no state to begin aggressive air operations as it was largely equipped with obsolete aircraft of French design.

Artillery spotting and tactical reconnaissance, together with limited bombing, were the standard duties of aircraft at this time. The types used in the largest numbers by the LFT were the Lohner B-category models, the Phönix-built Albatros B I, the Austrian Aviatik B I, B II and B III, and the Lloyd C II. An 8 mm Schwarzlose M07/12 machine gun, mounted behind the rear cockpit, was usually carried for the observer. By early 1916 the airmen of the Russian air arm were still flying generally

inferior types, but the Italian air arm was beginning to receive more advanced aircraft including three-engined Caproni bombers and French Nieuport Nie.10 and Nie.11 two-seat reconnaissance and single-seat fighter aircraft. The Caproni bombers started a programme of long-range day bombing raids over the mountains, which the Austro-Hungarians occasionally managed to tackle with the aid of a few primitive

One of the better fighters operated by the Austro-Hungarian army air service was the Albatros D II, this being a 53-series machine built under licence by Oeffag and powered by a 134 kW (185 hp) engine *(Bruce Robertson)*

Fokker E I monoplane fighters recently received from Germany for home defence duties. The Fokker's range was very limited, but its fixed forward-firing synchronised machine gun made it a capable fighter by the standards of the day. The Italians maintained their Caproni raids through the rest of the war against gradually increasing opposition.

Shortly before the outbreak of World War 1 Camillo Castiglione, a millionaire industrialist from Austria-Hungary's port city of Trieste, bought Hansa-Brandenburg, a German aircraft manufacturer. Ernst Heinkel, lately in the employ of the Albatros company, became chief designer of the organisation, whose products became a staple of the LFT. Probably the best of these was the Hansa-Brandenburg C I two-seater, which entered service in 1916 and became the most important aircraft of the *Aufklärungskompanien* (reconnaissance companies) for almost three years, with a number of subvariants characterised by uprated engines and more effective armament. Other reconnaissance aircraft that entered service during this phase of World War 1 included the Lohner B VI and C I, and the Lloyd C III and C IV. However, like many of the two-seat reconnaissance and general-purpose aircraft of World War 1, these types were generally inferior to contemporary single-seat fighters, especially after the Italians introduced the Nie.11 in the spring of 1916.

However, the LFT did not ignore the need to have its own high-performance aircraft. Austria-Hungary bought from Germany 39 examples of the Fokker B I reconnaissance type (later used as a trainer) and the MAG organisation of Budapest licence-built some Fokker D III fighters. Greater capability was provided by a third aeroplane type, the Hansa-Brandenburg KD (Kampf-Doppel-decker, or fighter biplane). This entered service as the D I and is generally known as the 'star-strutter' because of its unusual interplane strut arrangement. Two series of this aircraft were built by UFAG and Phönix, and several Austro-Hungarian air aces flew them. For a number of reasons, including the lack of an adequate synchronisation

03.09 was one of 12 Fokker M.7 biplanes that the Austro-Hungarians imported from Germany for service with the local designation B I a 59.6 kW (80 hp) rotary engine. This aeroplane is thought to have been flown at times by Offizierstellvertreter Friedrich Hefty, an ace with five confirmed and four unconfirmed victories *(Bruce Robertson)*

11

system, the Schwarzlose machine gun was installed not in the upper part of the fuselage to fire through the disc swept by the propeller blades, but was enclosed in a semi-streamlined casing above the centre section of the upper wing to fire over the propeller disc. This arrangement impaired performance to a certain extent, but the D I finally gave the pilots of the LFT a fighter with which to meet the Italian fighters on relatively equal terms.

Late in 1916 some 16 examples of a more capable German fighter, the Albatros D II, were licence-built by Oeffag.

Though still under the overall supervision of Uzelac's Kommando kuk LFT (HQ of the LFT), during 1917 the units of the LFT were reorganised along the lines of the army formations to which they were attached. At the lower end of the organisational chart, there were three main types of unit. The *Fliegerkompanie* (abbreviated *Flik*) was the basic front-line combat unit. Its pilot strength (officers and NCOs) was seldom more than eight despite the fact that the table of organisation called for a somewhat higher number. By the end of World War 1 the LFT had created a total of 77 *Flik* units. The *Fliegeretappenpark (Flep)* was the flying park responsible for supplying the *Flik* units with their aircraft, motors, guns, cameras and other supplies. The *Flep* units also undertook repairs that were too extensive for the *Flik* units but did not require the return of the aeroplane or equipment item to the factory. Each *Flep* was responsible for a fixed segment of the front, and the number of *Flep* units increased from three in July 1914 to 11 in November 1918. The *Fliegerersatzkompanie (Flek)* was the replacement unit tasked with supplying the *Flik* units with men, including pilots, mechanics and orderlies. The *Flek* was also responsible for the training of these men, and it was standard for each *Flik* to be assembled at a *Flek* and then despatched as a unit to the front. By the end of the war there were 22 *Flek* units, known collectively as the *Fliegerersatztruppe (Flet)*.

The *Fliegerarsenal* (generally known as *Flars*) represented a completely separate organisational strand of extraordinary bureaucratic complexity, controlled directly by the civilian-run war ministry. The *Flars* has responsibility for obtaining, evaluating and testing LFT equipment including aircraft, guns and engines. This organisation had existed since the beginning of Austro-Hungarian military aviation, but was not formally designated until March 1915.

In 1917 the *Flik* units were given a letter suffix indicating the unit's role, in addition to the unit numbers. The

The origins of the Hansa-Brandenburg KD's 'star-strutter' nickname are readily apparent in this photograph of a D I 65.68 with a 119 kW (160 hp) Daimler engine. Note also the casing over the upper wing for the 8 mm (0.315 in) Schwarzlose fixed forward-firing machine gun. This aircraft was on the strength of *Flik 34* (*Bruce Robertson*)

In May 1917, a senior officer of the Austro-Hungarian army casts his eye over an Oeffag-built Albatros fighter (53.20), the first D III from a line that had previously produced 16 examples of the D II. Feldwebel Johann Obeslo of *Flik 38* lost his life when this aeroplane was destroyed in action over the Romanian front on 14 October 1917 (*Bruce Robertson*)

Stabsfeldwebel Karl Kaszala, 18th on the Austro-Hungarian aces list with eight confirmed victories, was photographed late in 1917 while he was serving with *Flik 41J* (Bruce Robertson)

Austro-Hungarian aircraft such as this Lloyd C V two-seater of the 46-series, armed in the rear cockpit with a stripped-down 8 mm (0.315 in) Schwarzlose machine gun, were generally characterised by a clumsiness of design and finish. Note here the blocky radiator and associated 'plumbing' above the engine, and the lower half of the large fairing over the junction of the upper wing's port and starboard halves for the fixed forward-firing machine gun (Bruce Robertson)

letters were D for a *Divisionsfliegerkompanie* short-range reconnaissance and artillery-spotting unit attached to a division, F for a *Fernaufklärerkompanie* long-range reconnaissance unit, G for a *Grossflugzeugkompanie* bomber unit, J for a *Jagdfliegerkompanie* fighter unit, K for a *Korpsfliegerkompanie* for a short-range reconnaissance unit attached to a corps, P for a *Photoeinsitzerkompanie* single-seat photo-reconnaissance unit, Rb for a *Reihenbildaufklärerkompanie* photo-reconnaissance unit dedicated to overlapping photography for map-making purposes, and S for a *Schlachtfliegerkompanie* ground-attack and close-support unit. There were a number of other, comparatively rare, letter suffixes.

Once an aeroplane had been completed at the factory, it went through several steps before reaching its front-line operator. On completion, the aeroplane was inspected and passed by a Bauaufsicht, a specialist army officer attached to each factory. The aeroplane was then sent to a *Flars* acceptance group (*Gruppe I* at Aspern near Vienna, *Gruppe II* at Budapest, *Gruppe III* at Wiener-Neustadt, *Gruppe IV* first at Campoformio in northern Italy but later at Odessa for aircraft built by Anatra after the fall of Russia, and an unnumbered *Gruppe* in Berlin for German-made aircraft). The next step in the aeroplane's progress was despatch to one of the *Flep* units, and the final stage saw its delivery to a *Flik* unit.

In 1917 the LFT introduced a number of new and improved aircraft types. The Austrian Aviatik C I two-seater and D I single-seater (each designed by Julius von Berg), the Oeffag C II two-seater, the Lloyd C V two-seater, the Albatros D III built in Austria by Oeffag and, later in the year, the LVG-built Gotha G IV night bomber. The D I was built in larger numbers than any other Austro-Hungarian fighter in 11 series. Of unattractive but decidedly pugnacious appearance, and most commonly seen with a car-type frontal radiator, the D I was an effective fighter, but was hampered by a reputation for structural failure of the wings. Therefore, the D III built by Oeffag was preferred by most of the LFT's fighter pilots.

The Italian air arm sought to redress the technical balance with a number of more modern aircraft including three classic French types, the small but very nimble Hanriot HD.1, the improved Nieuport Nie.17, and the larger, less agile but faster SPAD S.7. By this stage of the war there were larger numbers of more diverse aircraft on both sides of the front lines. Over the Italian Front in particular ever-increasing numbers of aircraft became involved in more complex and costly air engagements. As always, it was the two-seat general-purpose aircraft, fulfilling the most important tactical roles of reconnaissance and artillery spotting, that bore the brunt of the fighters' attentions. Here the Italians were fortunate that their obsolescent Savoia (Farman) and Savoia (Pomilio) aircraft were

13

One of the mainstays of the Austro-Hungarian army air service's fighter arm was the Aviatik D I. This photograph shows 38.63 of the 38-series, powered by a 138 kW (185 hp) Austro-Daimler engine. 38.63 crashed as result of wing failure on 15 July 1918 injuring the pilot, Korporal Mazarlet of *Flik 74* *(Bruce Robertson)*

gradually replaced with more advanced types such as the SAML 1 and 2, SIA 7B and Pomilio P aircraft.

Drawing on the experience of the Germans over the Western Front, as well as the lessons of its own operations, the LFT in the field tried to create larger, more decisive fighter units, but these attempts were thwarted by shortages of fighters and pilots, and also by the reluctance of the army high command, which saw the task of the single-seat fighter as being the close escort and protection of the two-seat general-purpose aircraft.

Until October 1917, the fighting on the Italian Front had been relatively static with offensives in the Trentino region and no fewer than 11 increasingly bitter battles along the Isonzo river. However, from 24 October 1917 the Austro-Hungarians, with significant German support, finally achieved a breakthrough in the 12th Battle of the Isonzo (otherwise known as the Battle of Caporetto) and almost caused a complete collapse of the Italian army. The LFT was also heavily reinforced with German units. This greatly increased the effectiveness of the Central Powers' air effort over the Italian Front. On 25 October, for example, the German *Jagdstaffel 39* caught and destroyed no fewer than five out of seven large Caproni bombers.

British and French ground and air reinforcements were rapidly shifted to the Italian Front, and this helped to stabilise the position as the Italians recovered. The fighter units of the Italian air force were re-equipped with better machines, including the SPAD S.13 and Nieuport Nie.27, and as a result the Austro-Hungarian and German air arms soon lost their

Friedrich Hefty poses in front of a Hansa-Brandenburg C I (69-series) of *Flik 44F* on the Romanian sector of the Eastern Front in the spring of 1917

Some 24 examples of the Oeffag C I were built as the 51-series with a 112 kW (150 hp) engine, and of these most were used over the Eastern Front in 1915 and 1916 *(Bruce Robertson)*

The serial 03.45 identifies this aeroplane as a Fokker A III (Austro-Hungarian designation for the E III) monoplane fighter, the fifth of a batch of 14 such M.14 aircraft imported from Germany and seen here with the original armament of one 7.92 mm (0.312 in) LMG 08/15 fixed forward-firing machine gun *(Bruce Robertson)*

command of the air. By the end of December 1917 the recovery of Allied air power on the Italian Front meant that many of the airfields used by the Austro-Hungarians and Germans started to come under British air attack.

With their own last-ditch offensives on the Western Front planned for the spring of 1918, before the growing strength of the Americans could make itself felt, the Germans withdrew their air units from the Italian Front in March 1918. This left the LFT at a disadvantage, and the advent of aircraft such as the SVA-5 and SVA-9 meant that the Italians could undertake long-range bombing raids into Austria-Hungary, some going as deep as Vienna.

The writing was on the wall for Austria-Hungary, but Uzelac continued to try to provide the best possible equipment for his men. The LFT introduced five new types of aircraft during 1917 and 1918. These were the Phönix C I and UFAG C I two-seaters, and the Phönix D I, D II and D III single-seat fighters. Over the same period the Albatros D III and Aviatik D I were given a new lease of life by the installation of more powerful engines. Despite the faltering Austro-Hungarian war effort, the LFT was able to increase the number of *Jagdkompanien* from seven in the later stages of 1917 to 13 in 1918. However, this notional increase in fighter strength was more than offset by a reduction of one-third in the aircraft establishment caused by the decline in Austro-Hungarian aircraft production. It had been hoped that the Fokker D VII would be manufactured by MAG, and new fighters of indigenous design were placed in production, but only handfuls of these WKF D I and Aviatik D II fighters had been completed before the Austro-Hungarian armistice.

The other element of the Austro-Hungarian air capability was the navy air arm. This was smaller than its army counterpart, but

This Knoller C II (19.25) was built by Lohner as an armed two-seater with a 134 kW (185 hp) engine. The armament comprised two 8 mm (0.315 in) Schwarzlose machine guns – one trainable rearward-firing weapon in the rear cockpit and one fixed forward-firing weapon in a casing over the upper wing. This latter showed that Austria-Hungary was late in the development of an adequate synchronisation system, and that the system was not very successful in combination with the Schwarzlose gun unless the engine was running at maximum revolutions *(Bruce Robertson)*

was likewise hampered by lack of adequate equipment. Sundry Lohner flying boats, most notably the Type L, were used for coastal patrol and bombing up to 1916, and this effective aircraft so impressed the Italians that they copied it as the Macchi L. In 1916 the Type L was supplemented and then largely supplanted by the Hansa-Brandenburg K and KG, while the Type R (an improved Type L) was produced in limited numbers for coastal reconnaissance. The 'star-strut' interplane bracing arrangement also featured in a naval fighter, the Hansa-Brandenburg KDW (Kampf Doppeldecker Wasser, or biplane fighter flying boat), which was used successfully in 1916 and 1917 before being replaced by the Phönix Type A. Some 60 Phönix D II and D III land-based fighters were also employed for the air defence of naval bases. Production of seaplanes for the Austro-Hungarian naval air arm totalled 591 machines (13, 75, 102, 231 and 170 in the years between 1914 and 1918 respectively), and of these 304 were lost during the war (74 in action, 127 in accidents and 103 unserviceable).

Overall, during World War 1, Austro-Hungarian industry delivered some 5,000 aircraft and 4,000 engines – the poverty of this effort is shown by the fact that Italy, entering the war only 10 months later, managed to complete 20,000 aircraft and 38,000 engines from then until the end of the war. The maximum front-line strength achieved by the Austro-Hungarian air arms at any one time on all three active fronts was a mere 550. It is hardly surprising, therefore, that the army air service lost 38 per cent of its flying personnel killed in the course of the war, and that the equivalent figure for the navy air service was 20 per cent.

The Fokker B II (or M.17e2) was a German-built fighter and fighter trainer powered by a 59.6 kW (80 hp) rotary engine. Some 23 of these aircraft were delivered by the parent company This one (03.77) is being flown by Oberleutnant Fritz Bistrischan at Wiener-Neustadt during 1918 *(Bruce Robertson)*

Imported from the parent company in Germany, this is a Fokker B III (04.11), the first of 16 such M.18 aircraft delivered with a 74.6 kW (100 hp) Mercedes engine and complemented by eight similar aircraft (04.31 – 04.38) built under licence by MAG *(Bruce Robertson)*

RUSSIAN OPPONENTS

The primary opponents faced by the Austro-Hungarian air arm on the Eastern Front were the men of the Imperial Russian army air service. It was the Russians who made the first use anywhere of the kite balloon, when they used them for observation over Port Arthur in the Russo-Japanese War (1904–1905). However, the Russian development of an air arm operating heavier-than-air craft began in 1910, when the Russian forces established two flying schools, one for army pilots at Gatchina near St Petersburg and the other for navy and army pilots at Sevastopol in the Crimea. The Russian authorities also paid for officers to undertake flying training in France and the UK.

In the following year the Russian army held its first aviation competition at Gatchina for prizes offered by the war ministry, and later in the same year the army manoeuvres near Kiev in the Ukraine saw the limited use of aircraft, including Igor Sikorskii in his own S.5 biplane, for reconnaissance purposes.

At the outbreak of World War 1 Russian air strength was 224 heavier-than-air craft, 12 dirigible airships and 46 kite balloons. By 1 September 1915 Russian air strength had decreased to 145 before rising to 553 by the end of the year. The end of year total for 1916 was 724 before rising to 1,039 in March 1917 when the first Russian revolution overthrew the Tsarist government and inaugurated a socialist regime, initially dominated by Aleksandr Kerenskii.

The basic unit of the Russian air arms was the *otryad* (squadron) with a notional establishment of six aircraft, later increasing to 10 aircraft with a further two held in reserve. Later in the war the Russians realised the inefficiency of units as small as this, and three or four squadrons were

One of the best fighters available to the Russians during World War 1 was the Nieuport Nie.17, of which limited numbers were imported from France. This aeroplane is identifiable as a machine of the Imperial Russian army air service's 2nd Fighter Squadron of the 2nd Fighter Group, a unit commanded by Captain E N Kruten, an ace with seven confirmed and possibly eight unconfirmed victories before his death in May 1917
(Bruce Robertson)

batched together into groups. In 1917 there were four such groups: the 1st Group commanded by Captain Aleksandr Aleksandrovich Kazakov; the 2nd Group commanded by Captain Yegraf Nikolayevich Kruten (regarded by the Russians as their first major air tactician); the 3rd Group commanded by Captain I. J. Zamitan; and the 4th Group commanded by Captain Kulvinskii. The need for larger grouping of fighters had been appreciated before this time, however, and before the introduction of the group there had appeared a number of *istrebitelnyi divisyon* (fighter wing) units attached to each field army.

Flying on the Eastern Front, especially in winter, was most uncomfortable as shown by this photograph of Ensign Jaan Mahlapuu in his Deperdussin monoplane *(Bruce Robertson)*

The units of the Russian air arm often had as many as six different types of aircraft, making logistical support and maintenance an operational and bureaucratic nightmare. They were scattered very thinly over the great length of the Eastern Front, as were the opposing units of the German and Austro-Hungarian air arms. This dilution of strength, by comparison with the Western and, to a lesser extent, the Italian Fronts, made air operations much more spasmodic. Even when each side concentrated its strength to provide air support for land offensives, air activity was much less than that over the other two fronts. This is one of the reasons why pilots operating over the Eastern Front scored considerably fewer victories than those flying over the Western and Italian Fronts.

At the start of the war, the Russian air arm had equipment of similar standard to that of the other European combatants, but thereafter the situation deteriorated as Russian designers and manufacturers proved incapable of creating a succession of steadily improved aircraft or building them in significant numbers. Even after three years of war, with

The Imperial Russian army air service kept obsolescent aircraft, such as this Voisin pusher biplane, in operational use long past the time they should have been retired. Such aircraft were easy prey for any competent fighter pilot *(Bruce Robertson)*

The Anatra DS, otherwise known as the 'Anasal' was basically a scaled-down version of the Anatra D with a revised powerplant to improve performance. Even so, the type was not a match for the better fighters deployed over the Eastern Front by the Austro-Hungarian army air service. This Anatra DS was forced down behind the Austro-Hungarian lines, and may well have been pressed into Austro-Hungarian service with the local designation Anatra C I *(Bruce Robertson)*

Russia on the verge of the Bolshevik Revolution of November 1917 that was to take it out of the conflict, only comparatively modest increases in numbers had been achieved and these aircraft, with the exception of Sikorskii bombers and imported and licence-built types, were little more advanced than their predecessors of 1914 and 1915.

Although a few aircraft factories had been created in Russia before the outbreak of World War 1, the airframe and engine manufacturing companies failed to match the progress made even in Austria-Hungary, which was itself inferior in all design and manufacturing capabilities to France, Germany, Italy and the UK. Russian production of airframes in World War 1 totalled only some 4,700. A significant proportion of these were British and French aircraft manufactured under licence. An exception were the Ilya Muromets, a pioneering four-engined bomber designed by Sikorskii and manufactured by the RBVZ (Russko-Baltiiski Vagon Zavod, or Russo-Baltic Wagon Works) of which 73 were made. These included the S.16 (otherwise RBVZ-16), produced from January 1915 in one- and two-seat forms, the armoured S.17, and the S.20. Another comparatively successful Russian type that first appeared in 1915 was the Anasal two-seater, while lesser fighters and reconnaissance aircraft of the period included the Lebed' 9, 10 and 12. The Russian naval air service, primarily operating over the Baltic and Black Seas, made extensive use of seaplanes from the drawing board of Dmitrii Pavlovich Grigorovich: these included the M-5, M-9 and M-11 built by Shchyetinin.

Built only in small numbers, the Sikorskii S.16 was a small two-seater with side-by-side accommodation. It was built by RBVZ as an escort for the same company's Ilya Muromets four-engined bomber. While the aircraft was armed primarily with a fixed forward-firing machine gun operated by the pilot, there was also provision for a trainable rearward-firing machine gun manned by the other crew member *(Bruce Robertson)*

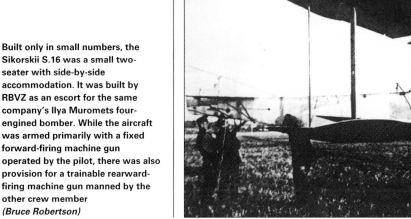

The Lebed' XI, of which only ten were built for the Imperial Russian army air service, was designed as a two-seat reconnaissance and artillery observation aeroplane, and clearly revealed in its design strong influences from the Albatros B-category biplane. Further development of the basic design were the Lebed' XII with a wing cellule of reduced span to reduce a tendency to 'float' and the Lebed' XIII with an uprated powerplant *(Bruce Robertson)*

The general inferiority of Russian aircraft is illustrated by the fact that most of the ace pilots flew aircraft of British or French design. The 12-victory ace Lieutenant Ivan Vasileyevich Smirnov (fourth on the Russian list) flew only British and French aircraft types.

Engine manufacture was in many respects even worse than airframe construction, and most Russian single-seat fighters and two-seat general-purpose aircraft were powered by imported French rotary engines, or the 44.7 and 59.6 kW (60 and 80 hp) Kalep developments of the Gnome rotary unit manufactured by the Motor Company at Riga. Larger aircraft were generally powered by imported French and Italian engines of the water-cooled type, most manufactured by Hispano-Suiza or Fiat. The standard Russian fixed gun for fighter use was the 7.62 mm (0.3 in) Pulyemet Maksima Model 1910, similar to the 7.7 mm (0.303 in) Vickers gun used by France, Italy and the UK. The first Russian interrupter gear was designed by Lieutenant Poplavko, an officer who had been working on such equipment since 1913, and was fitted to the S.16. Then in November 1914 an engineer named Smyslov and Lieutenant-Commander Viktor V Dibovskii co-operated in the development of a more effective synchronising equipment. Dibovskii came to the UK with a Russian mission in the winter of 1915–16, and worked with Warrant Officer F W Scarff (best known for his ring gun mount used in all later British two-seaters) to create the Scarff-Dibovskii synchronising gear, which was fitted to many early Sopwith 1$^1/_2$-Strutter fighters.

The Lebed' XII was an improved version of the Lebed' XI in the two-seat reconnaissance and artillery observation role with a wing cellule of smaller area to enhance agility and performance and at the same time to reduce the type's tendency to 'float' on landing *(Bruce Robertson)*

A French aircraft kept in service by the Russians long after it had disappeared from first-line service over the Western Front was the Farman HF.16, a two-seat pusher biplane with a sesquiplane wing cellule *(Bruce Robertson)*

Another French-designed aircraft that survived in Russian service much longer than elsewhere was the Morane-Saulnier Type L parasol-wing monoplane, pictured here in 1918. The wing was braced against flying loads by wires extending from the lower fuselage and landing gear, and against landing loads by wires running from the kingpost arrangement above the wing's centre section *(Bruce Robertson)*

All the major Russian aircraft manufacturing companies were involved in the licensed manufacture of French-designed aircraft. The Dooks (otherwise Dux or Duks) factory in Moscow built Blériot, Farman, Morane-Saulnier, Nieuport and Voisin aircraft. The RBVZ factory in St Petersburg (Petrograd after 1914) produced both Henry Farman and Maurice Farman aircraft. The Lebed factory in St Petersburg manufactured Deperdussin, Farman, Morane-Saulnier and Voisin aircraft as well as, in the period before the outbreak of war, German aircraft from the Albatros, Aviatik and LVG companies. The Shchyetinin company of St Petersburg completed Farman and Nieuport aircraft, the latter with a number of changes that adversely affected their performance and handling characteristics.

Most of Russia's imported aircraft came from France (Blériot, Caudron, Deperdussin, Farman, FBA, Morane-Saulnier, Nieuport, SPAD and

Voisin types), with smaller numbers from the UK (Airco, Royal Aircraft Factory, Sopwith and Vickers types) and USA (Curtiss single-engined flying boat types). The Russian air arms also used a number of captured German aircraft (most notably the Albatros B II and C I, Friedrichshafen FF 49, LVG B II and C II, and Sablatnig SF 5).

WAR ON THE EASTERN FRONT

Air operations over the Eastern Front were undertaken on a more limited scale than those over the Western and Italian Fronts, and were more directly linked to ground operations.

The bulk of the fighting on the Eastern Front took place in Poland, at that time the most western area of the Russian Empire. Initally the Germans and Austro-Hungarians were responsible for operations on the northern/western and southern parts of the front respectively.

The Germans were now faced with Austro-Hungarian calls for assistance. General Paul von Hindenburg, with the brilliant General Erich Ludendorff as his chief-of-staff, was sent to help the Austro-Hungarians in Galicia and also to check any Russian invasion of Silesia. In ten days von Hindenburg and Ludendorff moved four complete corps by rail in 750 trains from the German 8th Army onto the Austro-Hungarian left flank, near Kraków, to become a new 9th German Army. On 28 September a general German and Austro-Hungarian advance began.

As the Germans expected, Grand Duke Nikolai, commanding the Russian armies in Poland, was preparing a large-scale offensive through Poland into Silesia, the heart of Germany's mineral resources. The Russian plan was wholly unhinged by von Hindenburg's offensive. However, faced with overwhelming Russian forces, the Austro-Hungarians and Germans had fallen back to their original lines by the end of October.

The battle of Lódz in November was undoubtedly a Russian victory at the tactical level, but a strategic success for the Germans as the Russians were compelled to call off their offensive and, evacuating Lódz, complete a general retirement that ended any chance the Russians might have had of invading Germany proper.

The end of 1914 found the two sides on the Eastern Front in stalemate. The Germans and Austro-Hungarians reinforced their armies on the Eastern Front in preparation for a huge double offensive that von Hindenburg launched in January. The Austro-Hungarian and German South Army advanced north-west through the Carpathian mountains toward Lemberg. On its left the Austro-Hungarian 3rd Army was to lift the seige of Przemysl, and on its right the Austro-Hungarian 7th Army provided support for the principal effort. At the same time the German 8th and 10th Armies, under von

The mass of clothing worn by the pilot of this Nieuport 17 provides evidence of the winter conditions on the Eastern Front. This aircraft was flown by Lt Grajt of the 1st Soviet Aviation group in the border fighting against Poland, circa 1920, and bears an interesting personal marking

Seen with minor damage after running into a tree on landing, this Lohner Type C (C.51) two-seater was on the strength of *Flik 15* on the Eastern Front in 1915. The aeroplane carries the red/white/red stripe marking introduced in 1913, and later became a B II (U) with the revised serial 12.51 *(Bruce Robertson)*

This rare air-to-air photograph of air activity over the Eastern Front depicts one of the 24 Oeffag C I two-seaters that were built as the 51 series with a 112 kW (150 hp) engine before the advent of the C II (52 and 52.5 series) with 119 or 134 kW (160 or 185 hp) engines respectively *(Bruce Robertson)*

Hindenburg's direct control, advanced eastward from the Masurian Lakes in East Prussia.

Von Hindenburg's victory at the Masurian Lakes was not matched by the southern half of the Central Powers' winter offensive. The Austro-Hungarians failed to make significant progress in appallingly bad weather over difficult terrain. Their attempt to lift the siege of Przemysl also failed. The fortress city surrendered on 22 March after an investment lasting 194 days, and 110,000 men went into Russian captivity. Between March and April 1915 the Russians launched a major counter-stroke on the Eastern Front, pressing on into the Carpathians before they were checked by the South Army.

As von Hindenburg's army group kept the attentions of the Russians firmly focussed on the area to the north of Warsaw, a new German 11th Army prepared to make the major effort farther to the south in the region between Tarnów and Gorlice. The result was a strategic success. The Austro-Hungarian and German forces smashed through the Russian 3rd Army, retook Przemysl on 3 June and had crossed the Dniester river by the end of the month.

A new German 12th Army moved forward on Warsaw, which the Russians abandoned in early August. By now the Russian front was dissolving into chaos and it seemed that the Austro-Hungarian and German armies would be able to roll up the Russian forces as they fell back in disorder. The Central Powers' offensive ran out of logistical steam, after an advance of only 480 km (300 miles), on 19 September with the capture of Vilnyus.

Thanks to the efforts of the Grand Duke Nikolai, however, the Russian armies were pulled back in moderately good order. By the middle of September the autumn rains had turned eastern Poland into an impassable quagmire and the year's campaigning came to an end after the Central Powers had eliminated the great Russian salient in Poland to create a north/south front that now extended from Riga on the Baltic Sea to Czernowitz in the Carpathians.

Given the poor standards of leadership and the shortage of weapons, munitions and supplies with which his forces had been forced to contend, the Grand Duke Nikolai had achieved a miracle in preserving a considerable portion of the Russian armies on the Eastern Front at a time when there appeared every likelihood that Russia would

This Phönix-built Albatros B I (23.08) was the last Austro-Hungarian aeroplane to leave the fortress city of Przemysl before its fall to the Russians on 22 March 1915 *(Bruce Robertson)*

suffer outright defeat. The Grand Duke's reward for his efforts was to be removed from his command on 21 August and relegated to control of the Caucasus front against the Turks. Tsar Nikolai II took over personal command on the Eastern Front, and a poor strategic position was now poised to become worse. Overall, the Russians had lost more than three million men, of whom some 50 per cent were taken prisoner, on the Eastern Front in 1915. It is thought the Austro-Hungarians and Germans between them suffered more than one million casualties during the same period.

On 21 February 1916 the Germans on the Western Front started an offensive around the French fortress city of Verdun. This set the scene for some of the grimmest fighting of World War 1, and in March the increasingly hard-pressed French asked Russia to launch an offensive, near Lake Naroch, to force a diversion of German strength from Verdun.

The next major operation on the Eastern Front was also a Russian response to a request for aid, in this instance from the Italians, who were suffering heavily from the Austro-Hungarians' Trentino offensive launched on 15 May. The Russian offensive was planned by General Alexei A Brusilov, commander of the Russian South-Western Army Group and one of the ablest generals in the Russian army. The Brusilov Offensive was carefully considered and executed. The Austro-Hungarian 4th Army was effectively destroyed and the Austro-Hungarian 7th Army was completely dislocated. Brusilov received virtually no support from the other two Russian army groups on the Eastern Front, and he began to run out of ammunition and other supplies. A third effort between 7 August and 20 September brought his forces into the foothills of the Carpathians before complete exhaustion compelled a halt. By this time a German reinforcement of 15 divisions was hastening from Verdun to support the collapsing Austro-Hungarian armies.

Feldwebel Augustin Novak, photographed in August 1916 while serving with *Flik 30* on the Carpathian sector of the Eastern Front, achieved five confirmed and one unconfirmed victories to be 43rd on the list of Austro-Hungarian aces

This Nieuport Nie.6M monoplane of the Imperial Russian army air service was brought down and captured by the Austro-Hungarian forces in 1915 *(Bruce Robertson)*

Each side had suffered more than one million casualties, and the Brusilov Offensive had long-term effects. It ended Austria-Hungary's last pretensions to being a first-rate European power and hastened the collapse of the Empire. It also made inevitable the Russian Revolution of spring 1917.

Seeing the turmoil into which Russia had thrown herself, Germany

COLOUR PLATES

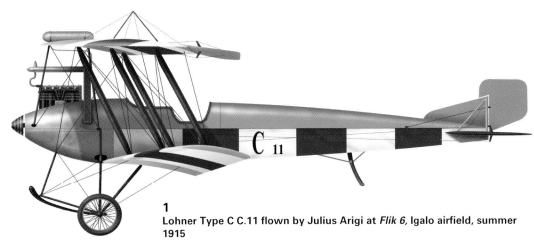

1
Lohner Type C C.11 flown by Julius Arigi at *Flik 6,* Igalo airfield, summer 1915

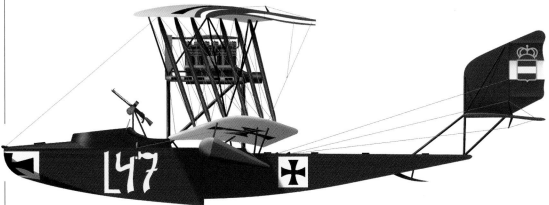

2
Lohner Type T L.47 flown by Gottfried von Banfield from the Trieste naval air station, June 1915

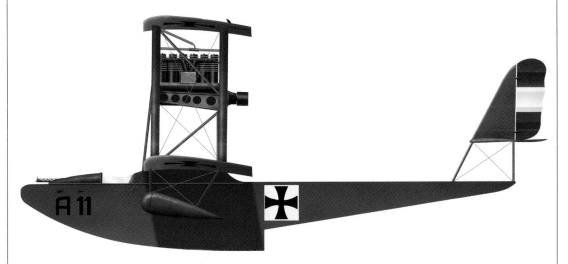

3
Oeffag-built Lohner Type H A.11 flown by Gottfried von Banfield, Trieste naval air station, 1916–18

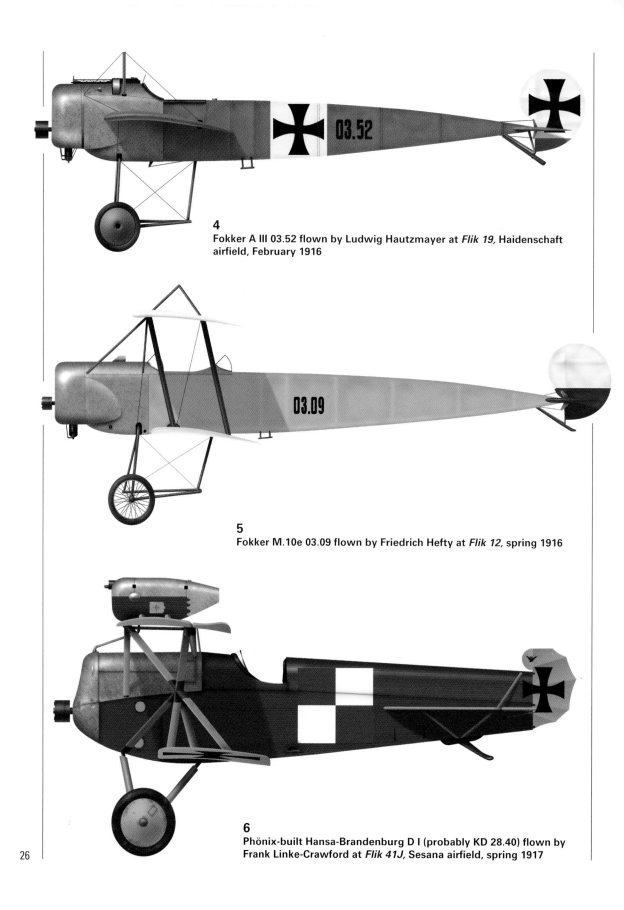

4
Fokker A III 03.52 flown by Ludwig Hautzmayer at *Flik 19,* Haidenschaft airfield, February 1916

5
Fokker M.10e 03.09 flown by Friedrich Hefty at *Flik 12,* spring 1916

6
Phönix-built Hansa-Brandenburg D I (probably KD 28.40) flown by Frank Linke-Crawford at *Flik 41J,* Sesana airfield, spring 1917

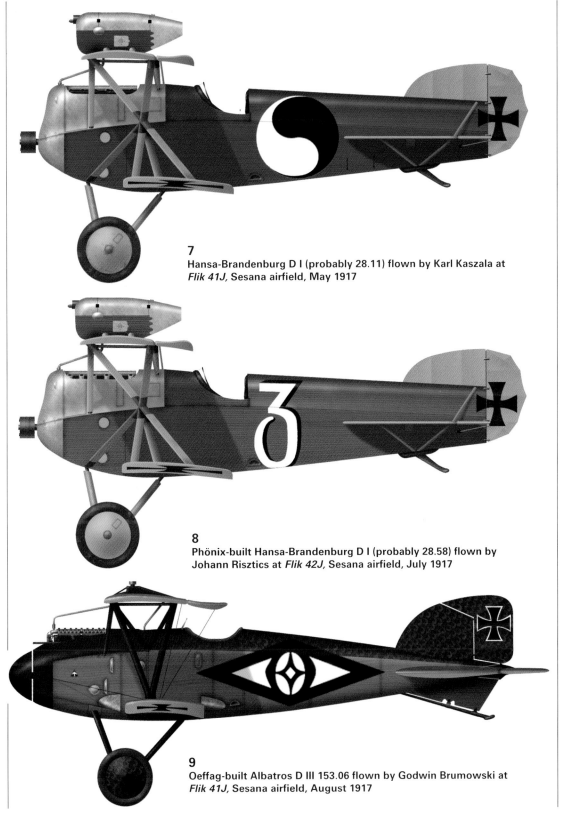

7
Hansa-Brandenburg D I (probably 28.11) flown by Karl Kaszala at
Flik 41J, Sesana airfield, May 1917

8
Phönix-built Hansa-Brandenburg D I (probably 28.58) flown by
Johann Risztics at *Flik 42J,* Sesana airfield, July 1917

9
Oeffag-built Albatros D III 153.06 flown by Godwin Brumowski at
Flik 41J, Sesana airfield, August 1917

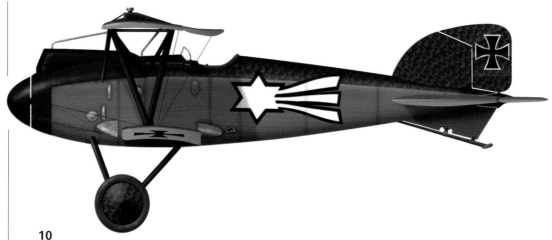

10
Oeffag-built Albatros D III (probably 153.12) flown by Karl Kaszala at *Flik 41J*, Sesana airfield, summer 1917

11
Oeffag-built Albatros D III 153.15 flown by Julius Arigi at *Flik 55J*, Haidenschaft airfield, September 1917

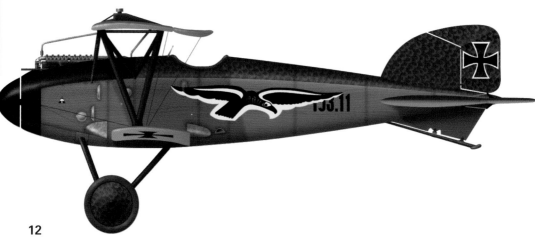

12
Oeffag-built Albatros D III 153.11 flown by Frank Linke-Crawford at *Flik 41J*, Sesana airfield, October 1917

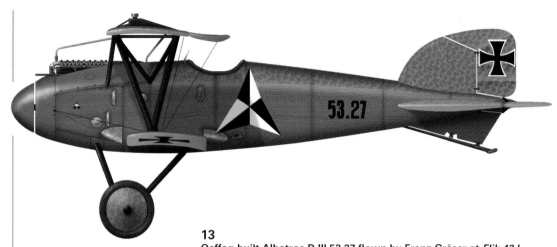

13
Oeffag-built Albatros D III 53.27 flown by Franz Gräser at *Flik 42J,*
Prosecco airfield, October 1917

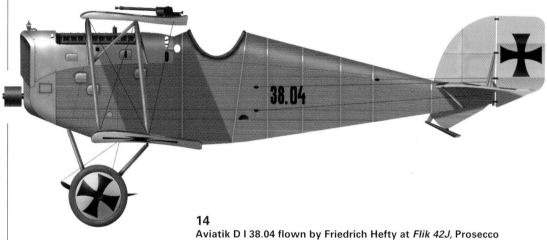

14
Aviatik D I 38.04 flown by Friedrich Hefty at *Flik 42J,* Prosecco
airfield, October 1917

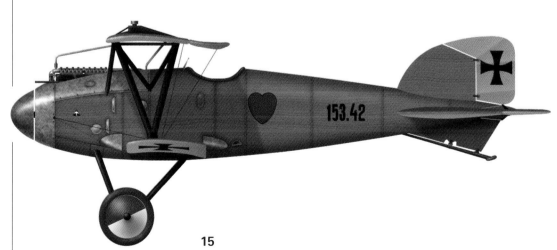

15
Oeffag-built Albatros D III 153.42 flown by Stabsfeldwebel Ferdinand
Udvardy at *Flik 42J ,* Prosecco airfield, October 1917

16
Oeffag-built Albatros D III 153.45 flown by Godwin Brumowski at *Flik 41J,* Torresella airfield,
November 1917

17
Phönix-built Hansa-Brandenburg C I 29.64 flown by Adolf Heyrowsky at *Flik 19,* Ghirano airfield,
late 1917

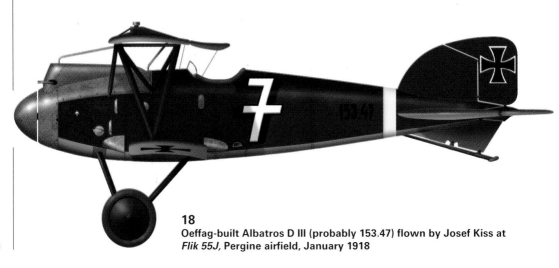

18
Oeffag-built Albatros D III (probably 153.47) flown by Josef Kiss at
Flik 55J, Pergine airfield, January 1918

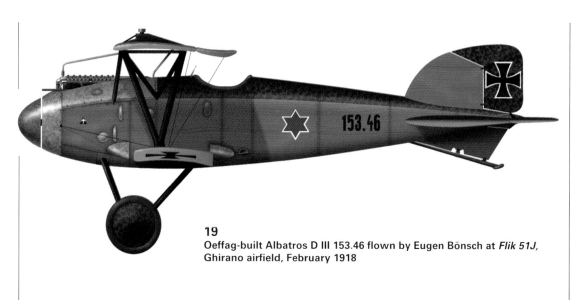

19
Oeffag-built Albatros D III 153.46 flown by Eugen Bönsch at *Flik 51J*, Ghirano airfield, February 1918

20
Phönix D I 228.24 flown by Kurt Gruber at *Flik 60J*, Grigno airfield, February 1918

21
Oeffag-built Albatros D III (probably 153.106) flown by Franz Gräser at *Flik 61J*, Motta di Livensa airfield, March 1918

22
Oeffag-built Albatros D III (probably 153.159) flown by Josef Kiss at *Flik 55J,* Pergine airfield,
April 1918

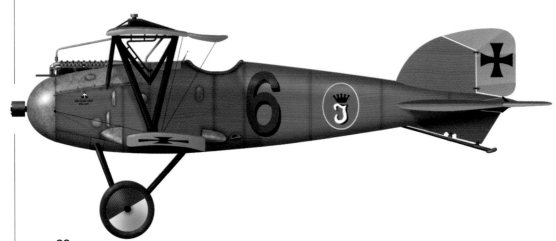

23
Oeffag-built Albatros D III 153.169 flown by Friedrich Hefty at *Flik 42J,* Pianzano airfield, June 1918

24
Oeffag-built Albatros D III 153.141 flown by Franz Rudorfer at *Flik 51J,* Ghirano airfield, summer 1918

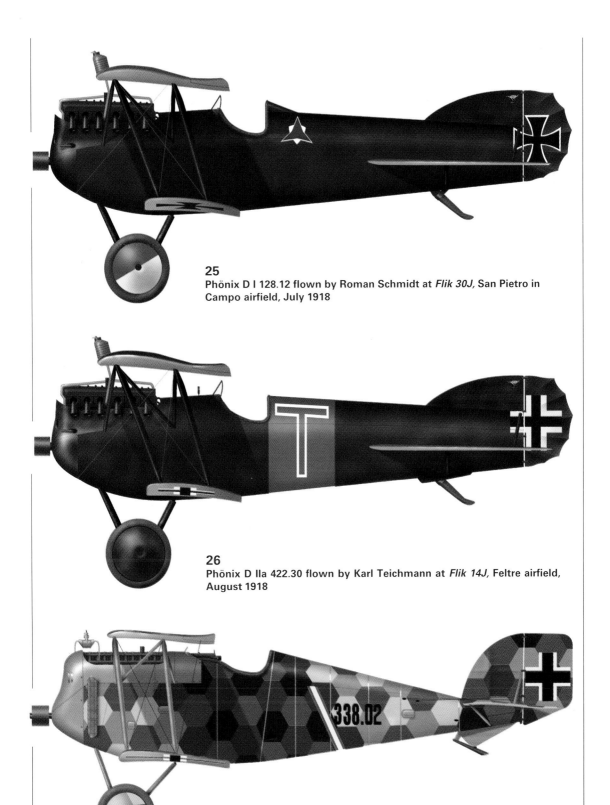

25
Phönix D I 128.12 flown by Roman Schmidt at *Flik 30J,* San Pietro in Campo airfield, July 1918

26
Phönix D IIa 422.30 flown by Karl Teichmann at *Flik 14J,* Feltre airfield, August 1918

27
Aviatik D I 338.02 flown by Bela Macourek at *Flik 1J,* Igalo airfield, Dalmatia, August 1918

28
Hansa-Brandenburg W.18 flown by Gottfried von Banfield,
Trieste naval air station, August 1918

29
Oeffag-built Albatros D III 253.06 flown by Friedrich Navratil
at *Flik 3J*, Romagnano airfield, August 1918

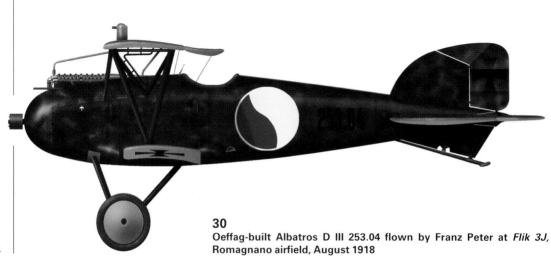

30
Oeffag-built Albatros D III 253.04 flown by Franz Peter at *Flik 3J*,
Romagnano airfield, August 1918

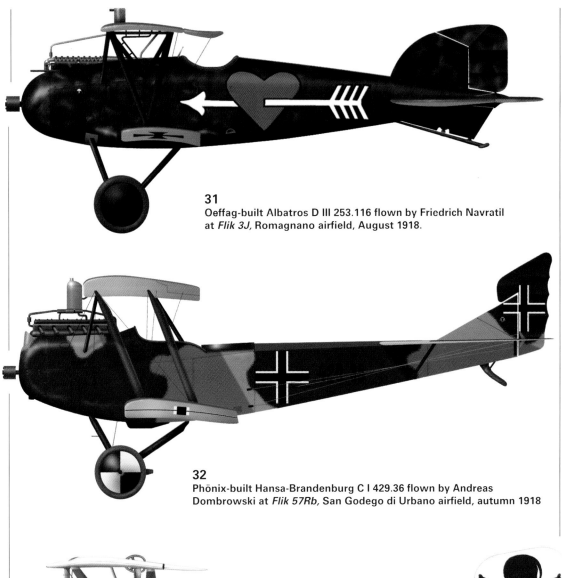

31
Oeffag-built Albatros D III 253.116 flown by Friedrich Navratil
at *Flik 3J,* Romagnano airfield, August 1918.

32
Phönix-built Hansa-Brandenburg C I 429.36 flown by Andreas
Dombrowski at *Flik 57Rb,* San Godego di Urbano airfield, autumn 1918

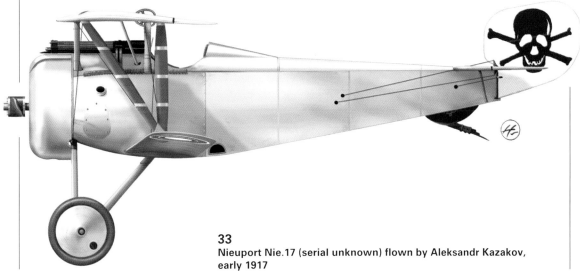

33
Nieuport Nie.17 (serial unknown) flown by Aleksandr Kazakov,
early 1917

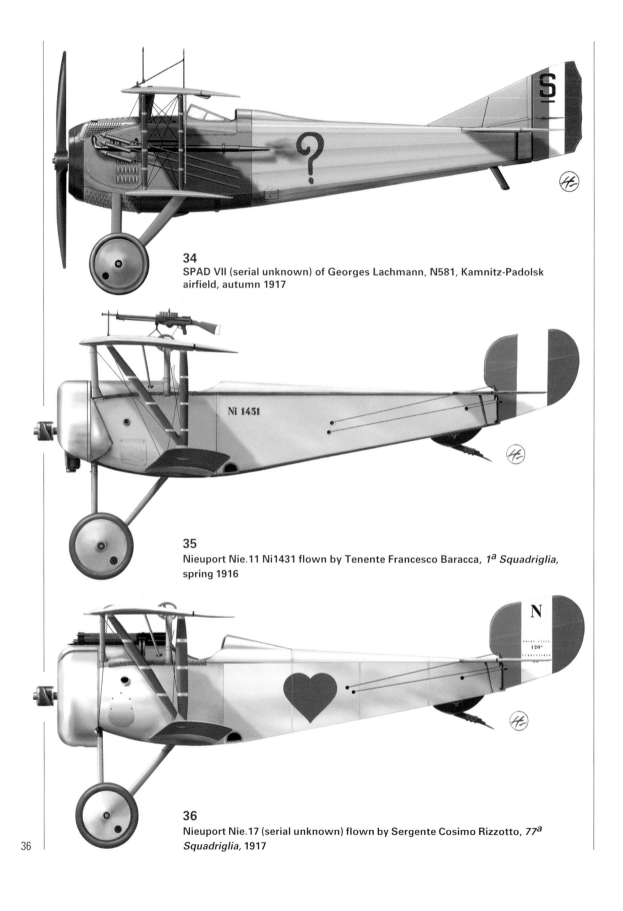

34
SPAD VII (serial unknown) of Georges Lachmann, N581, Kamnitz-Padolsk airfield, autumn 1917

35
Nieuport Nie.11 Ni1431 flown by Tenente Francesco Baracca, *1ª Squadriglia*, spring 1916

36
Nieuport Nie.17 (serial unknown) flown by Sergente Cosimo Rizzotto, *77ª Squadriglia*, 1917

Behind this Lloyd C V of *Flik 30* on an airfield close behind the Eastern front are visible an Oeffag-built Albatros D III (53.24) and a MAG-built Fokker D I *(Bruce Robertson)*

Oberleutnant Karl Patzelt, photographed in the early summer of 1917 while serving with *Flik 29* based at Kezdi-Vasarhely airfield on the Romanian sector of the Eastern Front, scored five confirmed victories and was 44th on the list of Austro-Hungarian aces

A pair of Fokker A III fighters, wings strapped to their sides to reveal red/white/red identification strips, are towed towards the front by a lorry of the Austro-Hungarian army *(Bruce Robertson)*

and Austria-Hungary (the latter now playing only the smallest of parts) halted all offensive operations and used the opportunity to redeploy major forces to the Western and Italian Fronts. Under pressure from France, Italy and the UK, now faced with the prospect of war against reinforced German armies, Kerenskii ordered Brusilov, now Russian chief-of-staff, to plan and lead an offensive on the Galician sector of the Eastern Front, and this led to the plan known as the Kerenskii Offensive or the 2nd Brusilov Offensive.

It began on 1 July 1917 with Lemberg as its objective. The Russians managed to break through the front, damage the Austro-Hungarian 2nd Army and threaten the strategically important oilfields at Drohobycz. Thereafter the Russian offensive collapsed from lack of supplies, exhaustion and increasing political disruption of the troops' willingness to fight. The Russians lacked both the will and the means to resist the inevitable counter-offensive, and the Russian front south of the Pripyet Marshes ceased to exist as the Germans finally called a halt on the edge of Galicia.

By September there was chaos in Russia. The provisional government, led by Kerenskii from 20 July, moved from Petrograd to Moscow as the Bolsheviks started to take over in Petrograd. On 7 November the Bolshevik Revolution brought Lenin and Trotsky to power, and the agenda of these two Red leaders in securing communist rule in Russia rather than maintaining the war against the Central Powers became evident with the signing of the Treaty of Brest Litovsk on 15 December. This took Russia out of World War 1.

A NEW FOE

Austro-Hungarian air operations over the Italian Front were undertaken on a larger and altogether more concentrated form than on the Eastern Front, because the threat to the Austro-Hungarian Empire presented by the Italian declaration of war in May 1915 was more immediate and at the time more threatening. This long, curved front extended from the northern tip of Lake Garda in the west in a great northward arc along the peaks of the Dolomite mountains to the east and then south-east to Caporetto before turning south to the west of the Isonzo river to reach the northern coast of the Adriatic Sea. In many ways warfare on the Italian Front was also more like that on the Western Front than the Eastern Front as static rather than mobile operations almost immediately became the norm. The Austro-Hungarian army and navy air services had to fight the Italians over land and also over virtually the full length of the Adriatic Sea. This latter contained all of the Austro-Hungarian navy's bases on its eastern side, while Italy had a number of bases on the sea's northern edge and western side, and also sought to trap the Austro-Hungarian navy by construction of the 'Otranto Barrage', a complex of minefields extending right across the narrowest portion of the Adriatic Sea between Otranto on the heel of Italy and Valona on the Albanian coast.

The first flying school to be established in Italy opened at Centocelle near Rome early in 1910, offering flying training for military as well as civil pilots. There was something of a sensation in Italian aviation circles during June 1910, when Tenente Savoia arrived in his Henry Farman III biplane at Centocelle having flown, in stages, all the way from Mourmelon. On 2 August of the same year Savoia took General Singardi, the war minister, for a flight round the airfield. By the end of 1910 some 31 Italian flyers had received their pilot's brevets, 16 of these men achieving this in Italy and the others in France and in Germany.

So good was the Lohner Type L flying boat used by the Austro-Hungarian navy air service that the Italians paid it the highly unusual wartime compliment of copying it as the Macchi L-1 to L-3. The L-1 differed from the Type L mainly in its three-bay wing cellule and the powerplant of one 112 kW (150 hp) Isotta-Fraschini V.4A inline engine, the L-2 introduced a two-bay wing cellule of slightly reduced span and area, a lightened structure, and the uprated powerplant of one 119 kW (160 hp) V.4B engine, and the L-3 (illustrated) introduced a new hull and tail unit *(Bruce Robertson)*

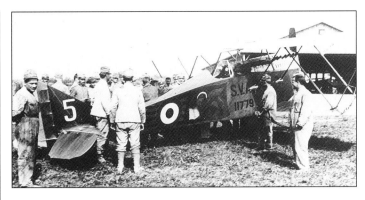

The Ansaldo SVA-5 lacked the agility for effective use as a pure fighter, but possessed the speed and range to operate usefully in the escort fighter and high-speed reconnaissance roles. As indicated by the 'Lion of St Mark' insignia on the sides of the fuselage (which was of inverted triangular section to the rear of the cockpit), this was a machine of the *87ª Squadriglia 'La Serenissima'* associated with Venice *(Bruce Robertson)*

One of the fighters much appreciated by Italian pilots for its handiness in the air and generally good performance was the French design, Hanriot HD.1. These aircraft were delivered in moderately large numbers from France, and were also built in Italy under licence by the Macchi company *(Bruce Robertson)*

Since 1894 the Italian army had been operating a small number of balloons and later airships, which were the responsibility of the Brigata Specialisti del Genio. It was under the aegis of this unit that in 1911 two military flying schools were established in Italy, one located at Aviano near Udine and Somma Lombardo to the north-west of Milan, and the other catering for civil as well as military pilots at Centocelle. The school at Aviano eventually became the major Italian centre of aviation. The school's initial equipment comprised five Blériot, one Etrich and one Nieuport monoplanes, and three Henry Farman biplanes. Of these ten aircraft, six (one each of the monoplanes and all three Farman biplanes) were committed to the army manoeuvres of August 1911, and were later despatched to the Italian colony of Libya as the 1st Aeroplane Flotilla of Tripoli.

The manoeuvres of 22–29 August near Monferrato witnessed the first employment of heavier-than-air craft for observation. Capitano Carlo Piazza flew the world's first operational reconnaissance sortie on 22 October when he reconnoitred the Turkish positions between Tripoli and Azizzia in a Blériot Type XI monoplane. Another Italian 'first' took place on 1 November 1911, when Sotto-tenente (2nd Lt) Giulio Gavotti dropped three Cipelli bombs on Tagiura and one more such bomb on Ain Zara from his Etrich Taube monoplane.

The success of aircraft in the Libyan campaign of Italian aggrandisement led to the establishment of separate naval and military air services. The naval service was named the Sezioni Idrovolanti (SI or seaplane sections) while the army service established on 27 June 1912 was the Battaglione Aviatori (airmen's battalion), named the Servizi Aeronautici Militare (military aeronautical services) on 28 November 1912.

By 1913 the Italian army could boast some 50 mixed aircraft operating from 13 airfields. At much the same time the Italian navy could muster some 14 seaplanes, and had established a flying school at Venice.

In the military manoeuvres of September 1913 greater use was made of aircraft for reconnaissance as well as observation purposes. One side deployed two squadrons, one of them equipped with five SIT-built Blériot aircraft from Cuneo, and the other with six Savoia-built Farman aircraft from San Francesco. The opposing side could also call on the support of two squadrons, one of them with six Savoia-built Farman aircraft from Pordenone and the other with four Macchi-built Nieuport aircraft from Busto Arsizio. The use of the aircraft was deemed to offer major advantages.

By the start of 1914 Italian military aircraft were operating from 14 airfields, with 13 squadrons and

One of several good types of
general-purpose aircraft developed
and produced by Italy in World War
1 was the Pomilio P series of two-
seaters offering good performance
and considerable strength
(Bruce Robertson)

two flying schools. As soon as Italy had declared herself neutral on the
outbreak of World War 1, there began a programme of intensive training,
concentrating on long-distance flying, and a reorganisation of the flying
service as the Corpo Aeronautico Militare (CAM, or military aeronautical
corps). As a result, when Italy entered the war in May 1915, her army
air arm was at a moderately high state of operational capability by the
standards of the day.

By this time the CAM had 72 pilots and 86 heavier-than-air craft in
15 squadrons, while the Sezioni Idrovolanti of the Italian navy had 15
operational flying boats and floatplanes, in the form of two Breguet, four
Albatros, four Borel and five Curtiss machines. The SI was not organised
into squadrons, and its aircraft types and strength were not well suited to
the support of naval operations.

By the time of the 3rd Battle of the Isonzo, in October 1915, the nature
of the CAM had changed. The emphasis of the Italian air effort had swung
in favour of the reconnaissance and bomber roles, and the sole genuine
fighter unit was the *8ª Squadriglia* equipped with Nieuports, at Santa
Caterina. This shared the task of defending Udine with the Farman
two-seater aircraft of the *2ª Squadriglia* at Campoformio, and there was
also a detached flight of Aviatik aircraft at Aviano for the defence of this
important base. The rest of the CAM's equipment at this time comprised
mainly Caproni and Voisin machines for bombing, and Caudron, Farman
and Macchi aircraft for artillery observation and reconnaissance. At this
time the CAM's only other true fighter unit was Capitano Chiaperotti's
71ª Squadriglia located at Aquileia also flying Nieuport aircraft.

Early in 1917 the CAM was reorganised to reflect the service's increased
size and importance. Each of the Italian armies now had its own attached
air element. The supreme command disposed of an independent air

One of Italy's best two-seat aircraft
was the SIA.7, seen here in the
form of an SIA.7B-1 with a 194 kW
(260 hp) Fiat A.12 inline engine for a
maximum speed of 170 km/h
(106 mph) *(Bruce Robertson)*

Francesco Baracca eventually rose to the rank of Maggiore (major) and secured 34 confirmed victories to become Italy's highest-scoring ace of World War 1. Flying a Nieuport Nie.11, Baracca gained his first victory on 7 April 1916 when he forced down this example (61.57) of the UFAG C I, one of the mainstays of the Austro-Hungarian army air service's general-purpose fleet *(Bruce Robertson)*

formation undertaking long-range reconnaissance and bombing from the Udine region, and the detachments of the Italian army in Albania and Macedonia also had their own organic air components. In the first months of 1917 the CAM comprised 62 squadrons, of which 12 were tasked with the fighter role with Macchi-built Nieuport single-seat aircraft.

By the time of the 11th Battle of the Isonzo in August 1917, a major programme to re-equip the CAM's fighter units was under way, and this was reflected in the fact that some units operated a mixed establishment as there were inadequate reserves to allow front-line units to be withdrawn for complete re-equipment: the *76ª Squadriglia,* for example, had three flights equipped with Nieuport, Hanriot HD.1 and SPAD S.7 fighters. Only 3 months later, during the 12th Battle of the Isonzo (otherwise known as the Battle of Caporetto) the number of fighter squadrons had increased to 15. In addition to these 'tactical' forces, there were 14 squadrons of Caproni 'strategic' bombers controlled mostly by the independent force headquartered at Padova, and 30 artillery observation and reconnaissance squadrons.

By June 1918 the SPAD S.7 and Nieuport were being phased out of Italian service, and the CAM's fighter arm was now equipped with the HD.1, the SPAD S.13 and the Nieuport Nie.27. Fighter strength in Italy was further boosted by the presence in the north of the country of three British units, namely Nos 28, 45 and 66 Squadrons of the Royal Air Force flying the Sopwith Camel and attached to the 6th Army. When the armistice with Austria-Hungary came into force on 4 November 1918,

Air operations over the Italian front were not the exclusive preserve of the Italian air services. The French were also involved, as indicated by this Nieuport Nie.23 single-seat fighter of the French *escadrille* N.561 based near Venice. The pilot of this aircraft was Sous-lieutenant Marcel Robert *(Bruce Robertson)*

the CAM had 68 squadrons. The presence of three French and four British squadrons increased Allied strength in Italy to 75 squadrons.

The first-line strength of the CAM in the operational theatre of northern Italy at the end of World War 1 was 1,758 aircraft. The steadily growing scale of the Italian air effort in World War 1 is attested by the fact that an industrial base that had delivered 382 aircraft and 606 engines in 1915 was able to complete 6,488 aircraft and 14,840 engines in 1918.

This classic photograph shows the Oeffag-built Albatros D III (53.33) of *Flik 24's* Josef Kiss in flight over the Alps in July 1917 *(Bruce Robertson)*

WAR ON THE ITALIAN FRONT

It was on 23 May 1915 that Italy declared war on Austria-Hungary. Italy had sat on the fence since the beginning of the war, thereby ignoring her Triple Alliance commitments to Austria-Hungary and Germany on the pretext that these two countries' acts of aggression in starting the war had voided the terms of the Triple Alliance. Since that time the Allied Powers had been encouraging Italy to enter the war on their side, their principal bait being the promise of Italian territorial expansion in the north of the country at the expense of Austria-Hungary.

The Phönix series of single-bay biplanes, here exemplified by a line-up of naval D IIs, represented one of Austria-Hungary's few successful attempts to create an effective fighter of indigenous design *(Bruce Robertson)*

The overall strength of the Italian army, commanded by General Luigi Cadorna, was about 875,000 men. However, the Italian army was seriously deficient in artillery, transport and reserves of ammunition, as well as the industrial base that would have allowed these deficiencies to be made good in a short time.

The Italian strategic plan was to undertake offensive/defensive action in an effort to hold the Austro-Hungarians in their salient (centred on the city of Trent on the Adige river) extending into northern Italy round Lake Garda in the region of Brescia and Verona, but concentrate their offensive capability in the east, where the Italians themselves had a salient that projected eastward into Austria-Hungary just to the west of the Isonzo river. The Italians' short-term objective was Görz (now Gorizia), to the north of Trieste, but the wildly overambitious long-term plans of the Italian high command envisaged an advance through Trieste toward Vienna.

Despite the existence of the Triple Alliance, Austria-Hungary had created extensive fortifications along the length of her mountainous frontier with Italy before the war began. The overall command of the Austro-Hungarian forces facing the Italians was exercised by the Archduke Eugen, while the potentially decisive Isonzo sector in the east was the responsibility of a force of about 100,000 men under the command of General Svetozan Boroevic von Bojna.

Although the Italians had been considering their offensive action for some time, it took a month for the final preparations to be made, and as a result the 1st Battle of the Isonzo only began on 23 June, lasting until 7 July. Under the command of General Pietro Frugoni and General Emanuele Filiberto, Duca d'Aosta, respectively, the Italian 2nd and 3rd Armies launched some 200,000 men supported by 200 pieces of artillery against Austria-Hungary's well-planned and carefully executed defences and achieved nothing in operational terms.

There were in reality no other strategic options open to Italy, and the result was a series of increasingly costly battles of attrition along the Isonzo. Fought between 18 July and 3 August 1915, the 2nd Battle of the Isonzo started after Cadorna had decided that additional artillery would provide the Italians with success. However, the Austro-Hungarians had reinforced the Isonzo front with another two divisions and held the Italians until their offensive stalled as supplies of artillery ammunition were exhausted. In the first two battles of the Isonzo, the Italians suffered about 60,000 casualties, and the Austro-Hungarians about 45,000.

The 3rd Battle of the Isonzo lasted from 18 October until

The airmen of the Austro-Hungarian navy air service found the Hansa-Brandenburg CC (otherwise KDW) single-seat fighter flying boat to be an excellent type. Flown in defence of the service's bases on the eastern side of the Adriatic, the CC was sturdy and, though less nimble than Italian landplane fighters such as the Nieuport Nie.11, was somewhat faster *(Bruce Robertson)*

Although Austro-Hungarian aircraft were generally armed with the 8 mm (0.315 in) Schwarzlose machine gun, crews were not averse to using captured weapons as suggested by this photograph: the observer/gunner's position in this Phönix-built Hansa-Brandenburg C I is armed with a captured Italian weapon, the Villar Perosa. This 9 mm weapon was the world's first sub-machine gun, and was produced by Revelli and Fiat as a side-by-side pair of guns on a common mounting and fired by a single trigger *(Bruce Robertson)*

Seen in Italian hands after it had been forced down and captured on 18 April 1916, this Lohner Type L flying boat (L.47) with a 108 kW (145 hp) Hiero engine and a three-bay wing cellule was the 'boat in which Gottfried von Banfield achieved his first victory on 27 June 1915 *(Bruce Robertson)*

4 November 1915, and began after the Italian forces in the sector had been reorganised and reinforced with additional infantry as well as a significantly higher proportion of the nation's artillery strength. The Italians attempted once again to break though the Austro-Hungarian front and take Görz, and once again were checked without making any progress. The 4th Battle of the Isonzo, fought between 10 November and 2 December 1915, was equally abortive. The 3rd and 4th Battles of the Isonzo had cost the Italians some 117,000 men and the Austro-Hungarians just under 72,000 men.

As on the Western Front, which had become a stabilised line from November 1914 at the end of that theatre's short initial period of mobile warfare, the Italian Front had now been provided with telling evidence that carefully sited and highly organised defensive positions were effectively invulnerable to frontal assault by forces using the weapons and tactics of the day. The Austro-Hungarian defence had been created and controlled in a masterly fashion, and the offensive tactics employed by the Italians can most charitably be described as inept, wasting the courage and determination that the Italian infantry had frequently revealed. Italy's grand strategic objective, namely the capture of Vienna via the Danubian plain and the Ljubljana gap following the capture of Görz and Trieste, was theoretically sound but basically impossible given the weapons and tactics available to the Italians in the face of the terrain and the Austro-Hungarian

This photograph of a Hansa-Brandenburg C I two-seater, possibly an UFAG-built machine of the 68 series, reveals the type of conditions in which Austro-Hungarian and Italian pilots had to operate. A wooden trackway leads from the hangar across the tyre-puncturing rockiness of Gardolo airfield, with a virtually sheer mountainside right up against the edge of the airfield. The aeroplane has two 8 mm (0.315 in) Schwarzlose fixed forward-firing machine guns in the fairing above the centre-section junction of the upper-wing halves, and a trainable weapon of the same type for the observer/gunner *(Bruce Robertson)*

Roman Schmidt is seen aloft in his Phönix D I (128.12) during the summer of 1918 over the Piave sector of the Italian Front

Friedrich Hefty poses in front of an Oeffag-built Albatros D III (153.58) of *Flik 42J* at the airfield of Motta di Livensa on the Italian Front during December 1917. The quartered red and white wheel covers were *Flik 42J's* markings

defences. At this stage Germany took no part in the campaign as it was not technically at war with Italy. This placed a strain on the relationship between Austria-Hungary and Germany.

There was a lull in operations on the Isonzo front during the last month of 1915 and the first two months of 1916 as both sides exploited the breathing space provided by the winter to create new (but hardly novel) plans and rebuild their forces. The 5th Battle of the Isonzo broke out on 11 March and lasted until 29 March 1916. The battle saw no significant change in the Italians' thinking or methods, and the result was another bloody draw that ended just before the Austro-Hungarians launched an offensive of their own on another sector of the Italian Front.

This Trentino (or Asiago) offensive began on 15 May and lasted to 17 June. Carefully conceived over a long period and then executed in a manner that caught the Italians totally by surprise, the offensive was based on a southward advance from the Trent salient by the Archduke Eugen's 11th and 3rd Armies. These two formations overran the Italian 1st Army under the command of General Roberto Brusati. The difficulties of the terrain and the steady arrival of Italian reinforcements finally halted the Austro-Hungarian advance on 10 May. The Italians then went over to the offensive themselves and the Archduke Eugen pulled his surviving forces back into prepared defensive positions. The Trentino offensive had cost the Austro-Hungarians 81,000 men including 26,000 taken prisoner, while the Italians had suffered more than 147,000 casualties including 40,000 prisoners, as well as losing 300 guns, and very large quantities of other equipment and supplies.

Cadorna then launched the 6th Battle of the Isonzo on 6 August. The fighting lasted only to 17 August, and although the Italians did finally manage to take Görz they failed to make the breakthrough that might have opened the way for an advance deeper into Austria-Hungary. The Italians were nonetheless elated by this modest tactical success, which had cost them about 51,000 casualties against the Austro-Hungarians' figure of about 40,000 men.

Between 14 September and 14 November 1916, the Italians undertook three more offensives along the Isonzo front: the 7th Battle of the Isonzo (14–26 September); the 8th Battle of the Isonzo (10–12 October); and the 9th Battle of the Isonzo (1–14 November). The battles achieved no further tactical advantage, and cost them 75,000 casualties to the Austro-Hungarians' total of 63,000 men including

20,000 taken prisoner. It did, however, begin to reveal that the Austro-Hungarians were beginning to reach the limits of their physical endurance.

The early summer of 1917 witnessed the revival of the Italian effort on the eastern side of the Italian Front, where the 10th Battle of the Isonzo raged between 12 May and 8 June. It had been agreed that this Italian 'push' would be co-ordinated with the British effort at Arras and the French offensive on the Aisne river (9–15 and 16–20 April respectively), which cost the British 84,000 men and the French, 121,000. German casualties were significantly lower. The appallingly heavy French losses led to a series of mutinies and ended, for the time being, any chance of the French undertaking offensive operations.

The Italian effort started well after the time it had been promised, and yet again the Italians tried to batter their way forward through mountainous terrain. The battle lasted for 17 days, and although the Italians made very limited territorial gains it was only at the expense of very heavy casualties: about 157,000 men against the Austro-Hungarians' total of about 75,000 men.

During the early summer there was fairly constant but small-scale fighting along the Trent and Isonzo fronts as the Italians planned and prepared for what they hoped would be the decisive battle on the Isonzo front, where they massed 52 divisions and no fewer than 5,000 pieces of artillery.

The result, between 18 August and 15 September, was the 11th Battle of the Isonzo. The strongly reinforced Italian 2nd Army, under the command of General Luigi Capello, drove forward in the region north of Görz, while on its right the 3rd Army under the Duca d'Aosta tackled the rocky hills between Görz and Trieste. The Italian 3rd Army was checked

One of the German-designed aircraft that saw service with the German units operating in Italy was the Albatros C III. This example was built by the Ostdeutsche Albatros Werke (OAW) and is seen after capture by the Italians *(Bruce Robertson)*

The major effort of the air campaign over the Italian front, as over the other fronts of World War 1, was borne by the two-seater types providing reconnaissance and artillery observation capability. This machine (37.40) is an Aviatik C I flown by *Flik 23D* from its base at Gardolo *(Bruce Robertson)*

This nicely posed photograph was taken late in 1917, with a captured Italian pilot, Sergente Malaspini, in the cockpit of Godwin Brumowski's Oeffag-built Albatros III (153.06) of *Flik 41J,* features from left to right Oberleutnant Benno Fiala, Leutnant Ickovic, Korporal Mayrbäurl, the captured Tenente Mazzarino, Hauptmann Brumowski and Oberleutnant Frank Linke-Crawford *(Bruce Robertson)*

With Hansa-Brandenburg C I (69.87) in the background, this MAG-built Fokker M.21 (04.65) single-seat fighter, known in Austro-Hungarian service as the Fokker D II, was on the strength of *Flik 37D* at Casarsa in February 1918 *(Bruce Robertson)*

in its tracks by the defence put up by the Austro-Hungarian 5th Army under General Boroevic, but the Italian 2nd Army on the left of the Italian front made good progress and seized the strategically important Bainsizza plateau. However, as so often happened in World War 1, when the infantry did achieve a breakthough, the advance soon came to a halt as the supporting artillery and the supply network failed to match the speed of the advance.

The Austro-Hungarians were now in trouble and had no alternative but to call on the Germans for major assistance to stave off the collapse of their defence. Germany reluctantly agreed, and this allowed the creation of a new notionally Austro-Hungarian 14th Army under the command of a German officer, General Otto von Below, with seven of its divisions and virtually all of its artillery provided by the Germans. The 14th Army gathered in the region of Tolmein, Caporetto and Plezza, and planned a radical change in the Italian Front through the use of new 'storm-trooper' style tactics. These so-called 'Hutier tactics' had worked well on the Eastern Front, creating in the Russian lines the large gap through which the German reserves could pour to exploit the breach, and would also work well in Italy as events soon revealed.

The potentially decisive offensive began on 24 October and lasted to 12 November, and is known both as the 12th Battle of the Isonzo and the Battle of Caporetto. The Austro-Hungarian 14th Army smashed forward against the Italian 2nd Army, which was taken by complete tactical surprise and could not initially react, especially as the Germans were using poison gas and smoke shells that threw the Italian defence into total confusion and prevented effective communication.

The Austro-Hungarian and German forces quickly penetrated the Italians' shallow defences, and it was 12 November before Cadorna finally managed to halt the Austro-Hungarian and German advance along a line linking Mount Pasubia in the north-west and extending along the line of the Piave river to the Gulf of Venice in the south-east. Italy had lost a considerable amount of territory but could now concentrate on the defence of a far shorter front, while the Austro-Hungarians and Germans had outrun the capabilities of their lines of communication and had halted. The Battle of Caporetto was a disaster for the Italians. They suffered 40,000 casualties and had 275,000 men taken prisoner, and in matériel terms they lost 2,500 guns and vast quantities of ammunition and other supplies. The losses of the Austro-Hungarians and Germans were, by comparison, a trifling 20,000 men or so.

Bearing the name 'Gretl' on the port side of its lozenge-camouflaged fuselage, this Aviatik D I (138.48) was flown by Oberleutnant Othmar Wolfan during 1918 from Pianzano airfield, the home of *Flik 56J* *(Bruce Robertson)*

Seen with a nonchalant cigarette-smoking pilot by its nose, this is an Aviatik D I fighter (101.11) built by Thöne & Fiala. The machine was flown by *Flik 7* in June 1918 and then by *Flik 9J,* and crashed on 20 September of that year as a result of wing failure, killing its pilot, Korporal Tomala *(Bruce Robertson)*

In grand strategic terms, though, the results of the Battle of Caporetto were less than happy for the Central Powers. Italy was able to rebuild her strength, and the Conference of Rapallo on 5 November agreed on the need for a Supreme War Council, the Allied Powers' first effort to create Allied unity of command. Meanwhile, Cadorna was removed from command of the Italians and replaced by General Armando Diaz.

In the spring of 1918 the Germans redeployed their divisions from Italy to France, which they rightly appreciated as being the decisive theatre, leaving Austria-Hungary once again to fight Italy on her own. If ever there was a need for unity of purpose, this was it. However, the Austro-Hungarian effort was bedevilled by the demands of General Franz Conrad von Hotzendorf, commanding on the Trentino front, and of von Boroevic, commanding on the Piave front, for leadership of Austria-Hungary's final effort, which had been strengthened by the arrival of more formations from the Eastern Front after Russia's December 1917 exit from World War 1. It was perhaps inevitable that the Austro-Hungarians should compromise. Instead of planning a single main effort based on overwhelming local strength with adequate reserves, they planned simultaneous Trentino and Piave offensives separated by mountainous terrain and with poor lateral communications: this made any realistic prospect of mutual support impossible, and meant that neither offensive had adequate strength or the reserves necessary for the exploitation of any breakthrough.

The Battle of the Piave began properly on 15 June after the failure of a diversionary attack two days earlier in the Tonale Pass, on the west of the front. The objectives for Conrad's and von Boroevic's forces were Verona and Padua respectively but, with notice of the impending offensives provided by Austro-Hungarian deserters, the Italians were able to lay an effective trap.

Conrad's 11th Army tackled the Italian 6th and 4th Armies and managed to make only slight progress before being halted and then repulsed by Italian counter-attacks in a process that effectively ended the 11th Army's part in the Austro-Hungarian double offensive. The forces under Boroevic, attacking across the lower part of the Piave river, managed to effect a crossing on a relatively wide front and penetrated the defences of the Italian 3rd Army to a depth of some 5 km (3 miles). However, rain then swelled the river and Allied air attacks broke the Austro-Hungarians' lines of communications to the Piave front, both of which contributed to the stalling of the Austro-Hungarian advance.

Diaz had kept the 9th Army in strategic reserve, and now used the Italians' lateral lines of communication to deliver major elements of this formation to the Piave front, where they pinched off the efforts of the Austro-Hungarian forces attempting to fight their way forward beyond the Piave river. Finding it impossible to get reinforcements from Conrad, Boroevic pulled his forces back during the night of 22–23 June. Diaz did not launch an immediate counter-offensive. This lack of action annoyed Foch (now Allied commander-in-chief).

Ground crew of *Flik 30J* begin to assess the damage to a pair of the unit's Phönix D I fighters (328.25 on the left and 328.30 on the right) after a bombing and strafing attack on San Pietro airfield by the Sopwith Camel fighters of the RAF's No. 29 Squadron in June 1918. The Austro-Hungarian aircraft were a mottled brown colour on their upper and lateral surfaces, and clear-doped fabric on their lower surfaces. Both aircraft bore the unit markings of white and red triangles on their upper fuselages *(Bruce Robertson)*

For the next four months, as the Allied forces on the Western Front contained Germany's last offensives and then went over to the counter-offensives that eventually led the Germans to sue for an armistice, Diaz was content for his forces to remain inactive as the Italian staff prepared a pair of integrated offensives. The Italian 4th Army was to drive through the centre of the Austro-Hungarian front while the Italian 8th Army, with support furnished by the new Italian 10th and 12th Armies (comprising mostly British and French divisions) was to drive its forces across the Piave river with Vittorio Veneto as their objective. Though such a division of effort can often lead to disaster, the Italians were now confident that they had little to fear as Austria-Hungary was teetering on the brink of total national disaster and already exploring the avenues that would lead to an armistice with the Allied Powers.

On 23 October, however, the Austro-Hungarian Gruppe Belluno showed there was still some fight left in the Austro-Hungarian army when it checked and threw back with heavy losses the Italian 4th Army at Monte Grappo, the key point on the centre of the front.

The Battle of Vittorio Veneto began on the following day. While the Austro-Hungarian 6th Army checked the Italian 8th Army along the line of the Piave river, the French troops of the Italian 12th Army, commanded by the French General Jean Graziani, gained ground on the left. The British troops of the Italian 10th Army, commanded by General the Earl of Cavan, secured a larger bridgehead on the right on 28 October and drove back part of the Austro-Hungarian 5th Army, thereby tearing a breach in the Austro-Hungarian front and reaching Sacile on 30 October. On 31 October Italian reinforcements began to race through the widening breach as the Austro-Hungarian forces collapsed. The Allies reached Belluno on 1 November and the Tagliamento river on the following day, while to the west the British and French troops of the Italian 6th Army reached Trent on 3 November. The twin offensives netted the Allies about 300,000 Austro-Hungarian prisoners.

On 3 November Austria-Hungary and the Allied Powers signed an armistice that came into effect on the following day, and Austria-Hungary was out of World War 1 just one week before the armistice with Germany finally ended hostilities.

This line-up reveals the Phönix D II and D IIa fighters of *Flik 55J* late in World War 1. Note the miscellany of fuselage markings among the unit's aircraft. The machine in the left foreground marked with a red heart and three white stripes was flown by Zugsführer Alexander Kasza, who would gain six victories *(Bruce Robertson)*

AUSTRO-HUNGARIAN ACES

The Austro-Hungarian 'ace' system was somewhat different from those of the other combatants in World War 1, and dictated that each member of the crew of an aeroplane that had played a major part in the downing (but not necessarily destruction) of an enemy aeroplane should be credited with a complete victory. Thus the pilots of two single-seat fighters involved in the shooting down of one enemy aeroplane were each credited with one victory, and the pilot and observer/gunner of a two-seater that forced down one enemy aeroplane were also each credited with one victory.

Given the fact that air warfare over the Eastern Front was undertaken on a considerably smaller scale than that over the Italian Front, and effectively ended in the middle of 1917, while that over the Italian Front lasted until November 1918, it is hardly surprising that most of the Austro-Hungarian fighter aces achieved the majority of their successes over the Italian Front. There were exceptions, who served on only the Eastern Front or only the Italian Front but nearly half of the aces served on both fronts at various times in their careers.

Typical of this two-front type of ace was the highest-scoring fighter pilot of the Austro-Hungarian army air service, Hauptmann (captain) Godwin Brumowski with 35 confirmed and eight unconfirmed victories.

Brumowski was a soldier of considerable skill and courage, and was also notable for his gift of leadership and his administrative capability. Born on 26 July 1886 in the village of Wadowice in the north-eastern Austro-Hungarian province of Galicia, Brumowski came from a military family and his education culminated at the Technical Military Academy in

Austro-Hungarian 'ace of aces' Godwin Brumowski poses beside the propeller of a Hansa-Brandenburg KD (or D I) 'star-strutter' fighter of the type he flew up to the middle of 1917

Photograph taken immediately after Brumowski's 20th victory reveals his Oeffag-built Albatros D III (153.06) with Brumowski standing on the left of the group by the cockpit. The cockpit is occupied by Sergente Ermanno Malaspini, pilot of the downed aeroplane, whose observer was Tenente Cesare Mazzarino, seen on the right of the group behind the cockpit. Standing in front of the aeroplane in light trousers is Frank Linke-Crawford, fourth highest-scoring ace of the Austro-Hungarian army air service

With a total of seven confirmed victories, Leutnant in der Reserve Otto Jäger was 24th on the list of Austro-Hungarian aces. This photograph was taken late in 1916 when Jäger was serving with *Flik 10* on the Eastern Front

Mödling, near Vienna. On graduation he was posted as a Leutnant (2nd lieutenant) to the Austro-Hungarian army's 29th Field Artillery Regiment, and at the outbreak of World War 1 Brumowski, now an Oberleutnant (1st lieutenant), was a regimental adjutant in the 6th Artillery Division. He served with this unit on the Eastern Front until July 1915, when he was assigned as an officer-observer to *Flik 1*, based at the airfield at Czernowitz under the command of Hauptmann Otto Jindra.

Brumowski soon showed himself to be one of the best observers serving on the Eastern Front and, flying as observer in the Knoller-built Albatros B I piloted by Jindra, participated in a daring action on 12 April 1916. Together with six other Austro-Hungarian aeroplanes, this two-man crew bombed a Russian military review in the city of Chotin on the occasion of the visit of Tsar Nikolai II and General Brusilov. The Russians ordered seven Morane-Saulnier parasol-wing fighters into the air to tackle the Austro-Hungarian aircraft, of which Jindra and Brumowski shot down two. These were Brumowski's first confirmed aerial victories, and were followed by his third on 2 May when he and his pilot, Zugsführer (sergeant) Kurt Gruber, flying another Albatros B I, downed another Morane-Saulnier parasol monoplane.

After receiving flying training, Brumowski became a Feldpilot (field pilot) on the strength of *Flik 1* on 3 July 1916. In November he was transferred to *Flik 12*, a unit serving on the Italian Front, under the command of Hauptmann Arpad Gruber. On 3 December Brumowski achieved his fourth victory when, in co-operation with Linienschiffsleutnant (lieutenant commander) Gottfried Banfield of the Trieste naval air station and Zugsführer Karl Cislaghi of *Flik 28*, he downed a Caproni Ca 1 bomber near Mavinje. This time Brumowski was flying Hansa-Brandenburg D I (65.53), which was newly arrived at the front and fitted with its gun locally.

Brumowski became an ace on 2 January 1917 when he scored a victory over a Farman two-seater near Lake Doberdo. Brumowski and his observer, Oberleutnant Julius Györffy von Telekes, were flying a Hansa-Brandenburg C I on this occasion. In February *Flik 41J* came into existence as the LFT's first genuine fighter squadron, and Brumowski was appointed as the commanding officer of the new unit. However, before assuming

51

Seen in light trousers as he gestures humorously at another non-commissioned pilot, Feldwebel Rademes Iskra, is eight-victory ace Karl Kaszala. The location is *Flik 41J's* airfield at Sesana and the period September 1917. Kaszala was one of only a handful of aces who achieved all their victories on the Eastern Front

command, Brumowski was posted briefly to a German unit, *Jagdstaffel 24*, on the Western Front to gain operational experience under the most advanced operational conditions available. This posting provided Brumowski with a keen understanding of the German fighter organisation and tactics. Brumowski was with *Jasta 24* between 19 and 27 March, and in this time flew four operational sorties over the Western Front as well as meeting Manfred von Richthofen, the rising star of the German fighter arm who in this period recorded his 29th to 31st victories.

Brumowski assumed command of *Flik 41J* in April and remained the squadron's leader until late 1918, and during this period many of Austria-Hungary's ablest fighter pilots (including Frank Linke-Crawford, Kurt Gruber, Karl Kaszala, Josef Novak, Friedrich Navratil, Rudolf Szepessy-Sokoll and, for short times, Julius Arigi and Benno Fiala von Fernbrugg) were on the unit's strength. *Flik 41J* was was arguably the best squadron fielded by the Austro-Hungarians.

In June 1917 Brumowski on two occasions flew the second example of the Aviatik D I fighter (38.02), which had been allocated to the *Flik 12* unit. Brumowski achieved four confirmed and two unconfirmed victories from May to July, but on 10 August recorded the first of a run of 'kills'. In the 9 days between 10 and 18 August, he achieved 12 confirmed and six unconfirmed victories. Much of this success was made possible by the increased pace and scope of aerial activity associated with the 11th Battle of the Isonzo (18 August to 15 September). Most of these successes were scored in what was arguably Brumowski's favourite fighter, the Hansa-Brandenburg D I (or KD) with the serial number 28.69. He began this string of successes with his tenth confirmed victory, a Nieuport fighter brought down near Chiapovano, scored while flying another D I. It was an oddity of the Austro-Hungarian system that there was a basic lack of equipment homogeneity in the equipment of its squadrons, and on 19 August Brumowski achieved his first 'kill' while flying an Albatros fighter: at the controls of an Oeffag-built D III (153.06), Brumowski brought a Caudron two-seater down in flames near Karbinje-Ivangrad for his 15th victory.

His first double victory was on 20 August when he was involved in the destruction of two Caudron reconnaissance aircraft, one while he was

flying the Oeffag-built Albatros D
III (153.06) and the other in his
Hansa-Brandenburg D I (28.69).
Just three days later, once again
flying 28.69, he co-operated
with Oberleutnant Frank Linke-
Crawford and Korporal Heinrich
Mayrbäurl to force down a Savoia-
Pomilio two-seater of the Italian
army's *45ª Squadriglia da Ricog-
nizione* as his 20th victory. The crew
of the Italian aeroplane, a sergeant
pilot and an officer observer, were

taken prisoner after their aeroplane had come down behind the Austro-
Hungarian lines.

Brumowski achieved his 22nd victory on 9 October, when he attacked
an Italian observation balloon near Isola Morosina. The balloon caught fire
but the crew escaped by parachute. This was Brumowski's first 'kill' in the
Albatros D III (153.45), a machine painted in the type of overall red colour
scheme he had seen von Richthofen flying on the Western Front, but
supplemented by a black-shrouded skull on each side of the fuselage and on
the top decking of the fuselage to the rear of the cockpit. This colour
scheme often appeared on fighters flown by Brumowski at later dates.

Another double victory day was recorded in 23 November when
Brumowski and Linke-Crawford together shot down a pair of Nieuport
fighters near the estuary of the Piave river, near Cortelazzo.

The winter of 1917–18 was comparatively uneventful, but from
February 1918 Brumowski was back in the thick of things, although
initially this was at the receiving rather than giving end of affairs. On the
first day of the month he was flying the Albatros D III (153.45) when he
became involved in a combat with seven or eight Italian fighters. In the
resulting battle the fuselage of the Austro-Hungarian fighter was hit by 26
machine gun bullets, and the fuel tank in the upper wing was also hit, the
escaping fuel then caught fire and itself ignited the cellulose-doped fabric
of the wooden upper wing and then the starboard lower wing. There was
little that Brumowski could do except break off the action and make for
his airfield while trying to avoid being badly burned.

Just three days later Brumowski was flying another D III (153.52) when,
in the region of Passarella, he was caught by what he described as 'eight
English fighters'. His aircraft was again peppered with machine gun fire,

the fabric tearing away from the port
lower wing and the spar of the
starboard lower wing being broken.
He was again able to make his escape
in his badly damaged aeroplane, and
made an emergency landing on the
airfield at Passarella. The aircraft
turned onto its back after touching
down, but Brumowski emerged
from the wreckage without major
injury.

**On 1 February 1918 Brumowski had
a major encounter with Allied
fighters in his Oeffag-built Albatros
D III (153.45). The enemy fire
punctured the D III's fuel tank and
ignited the spilling contents, the
resulting blaze burning away much
of the fabric from the Austro-
Hungarian ace's aeroplane**

**On 4 February 1918 Brumowski
came off decidedly the loser in an
engagement with eight British
fighters in his Oeffag-built Albatros
D III (153.52) and made a crash
landing at Passarella**

Austro-Hungarian 'ace of aces'
Godwin Brumowski is pictured in
the capacious cockpit of a D I (65.53)
'star-strutter' fighter with a 119 kW
(160 hp) engine. A unique feature
of this aeroplane, demanded by
Brumowski to reduce the number
of gun stoppages occasioned by
damp getting to the drum-loaded
ammunition belt in the upper-wing
casing, was the layering of the belt
in the upper wing

By June 1918 Brumowski had scored 31 confirmed 'kills', and his last four victories came during the final Austro-Hungarian offensive of World War 1 (the Battle of the Piave, fought between 15 and 23 June). He achieved his 32nd victory on the day after the battle's beginning when in the Albatros D III (153.209) he set fire to an observation balloon in the region of Spresiano. Three days later, in the same fighter, he scored another double victory. Near Passarella the Austro-Hungarian ace attacked and set another observation balloon on fire in the Val Grassabo, and later in the day he attacked an Italian two-seat reconnaissance and artillery observation aeroplane near Comtee to the south of Candelu, and sent it down in flames. Brumowski's last confirmed victory followed on the next day when he was flying a defensive patrol above the last intact bridge over the Piave river, which was needed urgently by the Austro-Hungarian ground forces. He tackled an Ansaldo SVA-5 which was attempting to bomb the Piave bridge and in a fierce engagement (the Albatros was hit no fewer than 37 times in the fuselage) brought it down over the Montello.

On 23 June Brumowski completed an uneventful sortie in the Albatros D III (153.209). This was the pilot's 439th and last operational sortie as either an observer or a pilot. On 25 June he was ordered away from the front on extended leave after achieving 35 confirmed and eight unconfirmed victories to be placed at the top of the list of Austro-Hungarian aces. On 11 October 1918 Brumowski was appointed to command of the fighter squadrons of the Austro-Hungarian Army of the Isonzo. As might be expected, he received virtually every award and decoration relevant to an officer of the Austro-Hungarian army, with the exception of the Knight's Cross of the Military Order of Maria Theresa, the highest-ranking but decidedly odd award for which one had to apply personally – Brumowski refused to do so. His decorations included the Order of the Iron Crown, 3rd Class, with War Decoration; the Knight's Cross of the Order of Leopold with War Decoration and Swords; and the Gold Bravery Medal for Officers, which was one of only nine awarded to men of the LFT.

After the war Brumowski was at a complete loss, and in 1920 moved to Transylvania to manage an estate inherited by his wife. He was temperamentally unsuited to the task, and also untrained for the work, so in 1930 he returned to Vienna and started a flying school at Aspern. On 3 June 1936 Brumowski was fatally injured in a flying accident at Schiphol airport near Amsterdam in the Netherlands.

Ranked second on the list of Austro-Hungarian air aces with 32 confirmed victories, and the only man to win Austria-Hungary's highest decoration for non-commissioned officers, the Goldene Tapferkeitsmedaille (gold medal for bravery) on four occasions, Offizierstellvertreter (deputy officer) Julius Arigi was a superb and natural pilot. Despite his success as a fighter pilot, however, Arigi remained a virtually unknown figure. He was born on 3 October 1895 in the town of Tetschen in Bohemia, and then lived in Marienbad until he volunteered for the 1st Fortress Artillery Regiment in October 1913. In March 1914 Arigi transferred to the Austro-Hungarian army air service and qualified as a Feldpilot in November 1914 with the rank of Zugsführer (sergeant).

Arigi's first posting was to *Flik 6*, stationed in southern Dalmatia at the notoriously difficult airfield at Igalo about 50 km (30 miles) to the south-east of Dubrovnik. He then flew operationally against the Serbs and Montenegrins in Lohner Type C (B II 12-series), Type H (B VI 16-series) and Type J (B VII 17-series) biplanes: of the B VII Arigi said that it was 'the first series aeroplane that was totally effective in mountains and, most importantly, an aeroplane that we, as pilots, fully trusted'. In October 1915 Arigi's B VII, flying a reconnaissance sortie, suffered an engine failure and he had to land behind the Montenegrin lines. He was taken prisoner but escaped in January 1916 on his sixth try; Arigi and five other Austro-Hungarian escapees stole the car of Prince Nikolaus of Montenegro and drove through the front line.

After the fall of the Lovcen fortress in Montenegro in January 1916, Oberleutnant Emil Cioll's *Flik 6* moved south to the airfield of Skutari (now Skadar) in Albania with a detachment considerably farther to the south at Kavaja, about 25 km (15.5 miles) south-west of Tirane. Conditions were appalling, with virtually no roads and several endemic diseases. To compound the unit's problems this theatre was the lowest in the Austro-Hungarian pecking order and the aircraft were therefore among the oldest and least capable still in service. *Flik 6*'s primary opponent in the air was the Italian *34ᵃ Squadriglia*, which was located at Valona and supported on occasion by longer-range aircraft from Bari and Brindisi on the eastern side of the Italian mainland on the other side of the Adriatic Sea.

On 22 August Cioll was informed that six of the *34ᵃ Squadriglia*'s Farman two-seater biplanes had lifted off from Valona and seemed to be shaping their course for an attack on the Austro-Hungarian naval base at Durazzo. Arigi asked for permission to intercept but was refused as there were no officers available to occupy the rear seat and, in the strictly rank-regulated nature of the Austro-Hungarian forces, serve as commander of the aeroplane. As the Italian aircraft approached, Arigi was twice again refused permission to attempt an interception. Then as the Italian aircraft passed over the airfield, Arigi took matters into his own hands and

Julius Arigi was the most highly decorated non-commissioned officer of the Austro-Hungarian army air service, and his tally of medals included four gold, eight silver and three bronze Bravery Medals *(Bruce Robertson)*

Photographed in the summer of 1917, this is the Oeffag-built Albatros D III (53.30) sometimes later flown by Arigi while on the strength of *Flik 6* on the Albanian front. *(Bruce Robertson)*

Julius Arigi was the second highest-scoring ace of the Austro-Hungarian army air service, achieving an overall score of 32 confirmed victories on the Italian front *(Bruce Robertson)*

took off in a Hansa-Brandenburg C I (61.64) with Feldwebel Johann Lasi in the rear seat. The two Austro-Hungarians rapidly overtook the cumbersome Italian aircraft and were later credited with downing five of the six aircraft in less than 30 minutes, although Italian records reveal that in fact only two of the aircraft were shot down while the other four managed to regain their base.

Arigi undertook a number of roles on the Albanian front, these including the sinking an Italian steamboat in the port of Valona (now Vlore) while piloting a Lohner B VII biplane.

Towards the end of 1916 Arigi was posted to *Fluggeschwader 1*, which was operating over the Isonzo front in northern Italy. Here he undertook mostly the escort role in the Hansa-Brandenburg D I single-seat fighter. He achieved his eighth to tenth victories in D I (28.06) and his 11th and 12th in a D I (28.08), all of them during April and May 1917. Arigi was unhappy with the directional stability of this fighter, which as originally built had a horn-balanced rudder but no fixed fin. Therefore, he designed a low-aspect-ratio fin and plain rudder that were installed on his aeroplane and later became standard. He was then posted to *Flik 41J*, but remained with this fighter unit for only a short time largely as a result of problems with the unit's commanding officer, Hauptmann Godwin Brumowski. Thus, late in August, Arigi reached a newly formed fighter unit, *Flik 55J*, located at Haidenschaft on the Isonzo front.

On 15 September 1917 he shot down an Italian SPAD fighter near Görz, in an Albatros D III (153.15); this was his 13th victory. In November 1917 *Flik 55J* was relocated to Pergine in the Val Sugana on the southern part of the Tyrol front some 115 km (71.5 miles) north-west of Venice. From this base the unit soon built a superb reputation for itself and received the designation 'Kaiser Staffel' (Emperor's squadron). Although the honour was accorded to the complete unit, it was often used more specifically for the flight that comprised the squadron commander, Hauptmann Josef von Maier (seven victories), Arigi and Offizierstellvertreter Josef Kiss (19 victories and the leading Hungarian 'ace'). Arigi achieved 11 victories with *Flik 55* while flying two Albatros D IIIs (153.36 and 153.80), at least eight of these were scored when Arigi was flying with von Maier and Kiss.

One of the aircraft types operated by *Flik 41J* was the Phönix-built Hansa-Brandenburg D I, and an example (28.67) of this type is seen here after a landing accident. Julius Arigi failed to score in the short time he was with *Flik 41J* *(Bruce Robertson)*

These three pilots were among the best serving in the LFT, and among their most notable feats were a 'triple' on 15 November 1917 when they shot down three Caproni tri-motor bombers near Asiago, and a 'double' on 17 November when they shot down one Savoia-Pomilio and one SAML reconnaissance aircraft south of Asiago. Arigi's first victories with the Albatros D III (153.80) on 7 December were another 'double'. By the time he was posted away from *Flik 55J* in April 1918, his score had risen to 25 confirmed 'kills'. He then returned to *Flik 6* on the Albanian front as a fighter pilot.

This Aviatik D I (238.82) was similar to the two aeroplanes Julius Arigi flew while he was serving with *Flik 6P* on the Albanian front *(Bruce Robertson)*

With this unit his 26th victory was a Nieuport downed near Singjerc on 17 April 1918 while flying an Aviatik D I (238.30). Then on 27 May Arigi, flying the Aviatik D I (238.51), achieved his last successes on the Albanian front when he sent a pair of seaplanes down into the water off Durazzo.

During the summer of 1918 Arigi returned to Igalo in Dalmatia as a member of *Flik 1J*, and received a pair of Aviatik DI fighters (338.01 and 338.02) for his personal use. In was in the second of these machines that Arigi achieved his last 'double' on 6 August when he was credited with downing a pair of Italian seaplanes. Arigi achieved his 32nd and final victory on the first of these two special fighters before being recalled to Hennersdorf outside Vienna to test aircraft built by WKF.

After World War 1 Arigi worked in civil aviation until 1938, when he became a fighter instructor in the Luftwaffe after Germany's annexation of Austria. His two most successful pupils were Walter Nowotny and Hans-Joachim Marseille, who achieved 258 and 158 victories respectively in World War 2. Arigi died peacefully on 1 August 1981.

The third ranking Austro-Hungarian ace, Oberleutnant in der Reserve Benno Fiala, Ritter von Fernbrugg, is a classic example of the 'total aviation person' in the early days of European aviation. Fiala was a man of intelligence, far-sightedness, bravery, flying skill and administrative capability, and in the course of a career lasting some 40 years he became involved in areas of aviation as diverse as air fighting, airline establishment, airport management and aircraft manufacturing. It was in the first of these fields that he is best remembered, for as the third-ranking ace of the LFT he scored a total of 28 confirmed and five unconfirmed victories during World War 1.

Fiala was born on 16 June 1890 into a Viennese family with strong links to the Austro-Hungarian military. Fiala's education ended at the Technical University in Vienna, where he gained the title of Ingenieur (engineer). He volunteered for military service in 1910 and was assigned as an Offizieranwärter (officer candidate) to the 1st Artillery Regiment. His subsequent involvement in flying stemmed from two things: firstly, his brother Otto, a Fregattenleutnant (lieutenant in the navy) and one of the first pilots of the fledgling naval air service, fed his younger brother with accounts of flying; and secondly, he had a fortuitous meeting with

Named 'Durch', this is the Aviatik B I of *Flik 1* in which Benno Fiala served his apprenticeship in the Eastern Front late in 1914. The airfield was located at Brzesko, and the aeroplane carries the original type of national markings, namely red/white/red stripes, here evident on the sides of the fuselage. Benno Fiala is visible in the front cockpit

Oberstleutnant (lieutenant colonel) Emil Uzelac, commander of the Army Airship Section – the small unit that was later expanded into the LFT – who further stirred his growing fascination with flight. On the eve of World War 1, Fiala successfully applied, via Uzelac, for a transfer from the artillery to the LFT, and on 28 July 1914 Fiala was posted to *Fliegerkompanie 1*.

At the outbreak of war, *Flik 1* was assigned to the Galician theatre on the Eastern Front. Fiala travelled to this theatre as the unit's technical officer, although it was not long before he took to the air as an observer. On 31 July 1914 he was the observer for *Flik 1*'s first wartime sortie, in a Lohner B III with Apparatchauffeur Erdstein. (It was standard practice at this time for a non-commissioned officer to fly the aeroplane almost as a chauffeur for the officer, who was entrusted with the more important task of tactical

28.48 was a highly modified Phönix-built Hansa-Brandenburg D I. Its alterations were inspired by the sesquiplane configuration of the Nieuport. The fuselage was raised to the level of the enlarged upper wing, and a narrow lower wing was fitted, supported by a single V-strut and a slanted brace connected to the fuselage. It was test flown by Hauptmann Karl Nikitsch, who crashed it on 16 January 1917. It was rebuilt as 20.14, but the type was not selected for production (*Bruce Robertson*)

Third on the list of Austro-Hungarian aces, Oberleutnant in der Reserve Benno Fiala, Ritter von Fernbrugg, was credited with 28 confirmed and five unconfirmed victories. He is depicted here in front of his Phönix-built Hansa-Brandenburg KD (D I serialled 28.38) of *Flik 12D* in the autumn of 1917. Fiala achieved five of his victories in this aeroplane

reconnaissance and should not soil his hands with the mechanical aspect of flying.) Fiala took every opportunity to exploit his capacity for inventiveness and he soon appreciated that artillery observation would be considerably enhanced if the observer had a means of relaying information to the relevant artillery units as soon as it became available, and therefore installed a radio transmitter in one (later several) of the unit's aircraft. Fiala was also important in the introduction of machine guns and reconnaissance cameras in the cockpits of the unit's aircraft.

Fiala then began to reveal the courage that was to typify his career. In August 1914 he was on a train carrying aircraft and supplies for *Flik 1*. When the train was in the region of Czortków, a large body of Russian troops ambushed it after breaking through the lines. In the bout of firing the train's engineer was badly wounded and the train came to a stop. Fiala leapt out of the train and past the advancing Russians to brave a hail of fire and reach the cab of the locomotive. Despite the fact that had had been wounded, Fiala managed to get the train moving and soon outdistanced the Russians. For this feat he received an extraordinary promotion (out of sequence, which was a notably rare event in the seniority-based promotion ladder of the Austro-Hungarian army) to Leutnant in der Reserve (reserve 2nd lieutenant) on 10 November 1914.

The success of his numerous flights as an observer (later observer gunner) led to the award of the Silver Military Merit Medal, whose citation mentions the fact that Fiala shot down Russian aircraft on 6 and 13 June 1915. No further confirmation of these victories has ever been found. After a brief detachment to the experimental testing section of the Luftfahrt-Arsenals (air arsenal), a detachment reflecting Fiala's capability in the engineering and development aspects of military aviation, he was posted as an observer gunner to the new *Flik 19* in January 1916. Commanded by the able Hauptmann Adolf Heyrowsky, this unit was based at Haidenschaft airfield in the Wippach valley on the Isonzo front in north-eastern Italy, and came to be regarded as the best two-seater unit in the LFT. In common with other LFT units, *Flik 19* had on its strength a number of different two-seat aircraft types, although the 'standard' type was the Hansa-Brandenburg C I in several of its series. The unit was tasked with the full range of two-seater duties including photo-reconnaissance, artillery spotting, communication, liaison and even, on occasion, ground attack.

It was with *Flik 19* that Fiala achieved his first confirmed victory. On 29 April 1916 he was the observer gunner of a two-seater piloted by Leutnant Ludwig Hautzmayer, and the fire of his machine gun severely damaged an Italian two-seater that crash landed near San Daniele. On 4 May of the same year he had his next success. Flying in a Hansa-Brandenburg C I (61.55) piloted by Heyrowsky, he tackled the Italian airship M.4, cruising over Merna near Gorizia, with explosive ammunition specifically designed for use against lighter-than-air craft. Soon the airship was ablaze and it fell to the ground by the road linking Gorizia with Merna, resulting in the death of the airship's six-man crew.

Fiala's time with *Flik 19* ended in the course of a bombing sortie against a target heavily protected by anti-aircraft guns early in 1917. During the attack, Fiala was badly wounded in the right arm by a shell fragment. On return to base, he was hospitalised and then, during his recuperation,

Seen here with the Erzherzogin Maria Theresia are (left) Godwin Brumowski and (right) Benno Fiala. The occasion was a royal visit to *Flik 41J's* airfield at Sesana on 26 July 1917

decided to become a pilot. With his wound healed and the relevant authorisation granted, he arrived at a flying school that specialised in the fighter pilot training. Fiala proved to be a natural pilot, and his training proceeded with only one incident. This occurred on 11 May when the engine of his aeroplane failed and, in the ensuing crash landing, he broke his collar bone. He soon recovered and completed his training without further ado.

At the end of June, Fiala was assigned to *Flik 41J*, a celebrated fighter unit, but a mere five weeks later he was posted to *Flik 12D*, a unit that was thought to need an injection of new yet experienced 'blood'. Commanded by Hauptmann Arpad Gruber, *Flik 12D* was in essence a two-seater unit but had several single-seat fighters on its strength to provide escort for the two-seat machines. The type most frequently flown by Fiala was the Hansa-Brandenburg D I (otherwise known as KD), which was fast but tricky to handle as it was notoriously unstable. Fiala was a pilot able to overcome the limitations of the D I and at the same time exploit its capabilities, and the result was a steadily growing list of successes. In his first 23 days with *Flik 12D*, for example, Fiala achieved seven air-to-air 'kills'. On 10 August, flying D I (28.38), he despatched a Caproni bomber behind enemy lines in the vicinity of Auzza-Plava. On the following day, in the same aeroplane, he shot down a SAML two-seat reconnaissance aeroplane in flames, and it fell behind the Italian lines. Confirmation by Austro-Hungarian ground forces gave him his fifth confirmed victory and made him an ace. On 19 August, again in the same aeroplane, Fiala set fire to a Caproni bomber, which crashed just to the rear of the Italian lines near Fajti Hrib.

Fiala ended his scoring at *Flik 12D* on 25 October when he tackled an Italian SPAD S.7 fighter in his D I (28.38) just to the south of Monte San Gabriele, and gained his eighth confirmed victory. During his time at *Flik 12D*, Fiala received two significant decorations, first the Order of the Iron Crown, 3rd Class, with War Decoration and Swords, and then the Knight's Cross of the Order of Leopold, with War Decoration and Swords: he was one of only 25 LFT officers to receive this latter decoration.

During November Fiala was posted as deputy commanding officer to a genuine fighter unit, *Flik 56J* led by Hauptmann Robert Ellner. Fiala's time with this squadron was relatively uneventful except for one 'kill' scored on 30 December. Piloting an Albatros D III (153.77), he intercepted a Caproni bomber near Vecchia in the region of Susegana and, after a difficult engagement, shot down the bomber in flames.

It was at the end of January 1918 that Fiala finally received the posting that would allow him to make best use of his talents, both operational and administrative, when he was appointed to the command of *Flik 51J*, a high-quality fighter unit that included, in addition to Fiala himself, five other aces. *Flik 51J* flew the Albatros D III in its licence-built Series 153 and 253 forms. The operational remit of *Flik 51J* was the full range of fighter activities, including interception, escort, ground attack and light attack of ground targets with small bombs.

On 11 March, flying D III (153.128), Fiala shot down a Sopwith Camel that reached the ground near Spresiano at an acute angle and somersaulted before coming apart. Flying the same aeroplane two days later, Fiala encountered an SIA 7B two-seater carrying small bombs for attacks on

In common with a number of other aircraft designed and built in Austria-Hungary, the Knoller B I two-seater had a high forward decking over its inline engine, in this instance a Thöne & Fiala-built training machine in the 35.8-series with a 74.6 kW (100 hp) engine. In combination with the large windscreen, this provided the crew with good protection from the slipstream *(Bruce Robertson)*

Portraits and photographs of Frank Linke-Crawford generally reveal a man of serious appearance *(Bruce Robertson)*

targets of opportunity. Fiala shot down the Italian aeroplane, which hit the ground north of Spresiano, with a vivid explosion as the bombs and the remaining petrol went off. On 30 March, flying D III (153.155), Fiala claimed his 14th victory when he forced down a Sopwith Camel near Gorge del Molino. The British fighter overturned on landing and was destroyed. The pilot was Lieutenant Allan Jerrard of No. 66 Squadron, Royal Flying Corps, who was later awarded the Victoria Cross for his conduct in this fight.

1 May was a great day in Fiala's career as a fighter pilot. Flying D III (153.128), he shot down a Camel behind the Allied lines. He then fell in with an SIA 7B which he shot down north of Povegliano, and moved on to attack an Italian observation balloon that went down in flames near Visnadello. Returning to his starting point near San Biaggio, he shot down another observation balloon to complete four victories in a single sortie.

On 6 June Fiala was flying a D III (153.128) when he met a SPAD fighter of the Italian air arm over Salettual-Roncadelle and shot it down. Later in the same day, and flying the same fighter, he shot down a Camel over Noventa di Piave as his 21st confirmed victory. Just under a fortnight later he was less fortunate when, during a sortie to machine gun and bomb Allied entrenchments, he was hit by machine gun or rifle fire and received two wounds in his right hand. Receiving medical attention at his unit's airfield, Fiala decided against hospitalisation or ground duty. Three days later, with his hand still heavily bandaged, Fiala took off in one of eight D III fighters which *Flik 51J* contributed to the major engagement that became known as the 'Air Battle over the Montello'. The aircraft of *Flik 51J* attacked an Allied force of 10 bombers escorted by 16 fighters. *Flik 51J*'s fighters shot down five Allied aircraft in a swirling dogfight, suffering no losses themselves. During this engagement, in which he was flying D III (153.270), Fiala was responsible for three of the 'kills'.

Fiala achieved his last success in air combat on 20 August, when he shot down an SVA-5 high-speed reconnaissance aeroplane to the south of Papadopoli Island near Cissalto. He flew operationally until early October, when he was posted to a bureaucratic job in Vienna on the staff of the LFT's inspector general. Fiala ended the war with 28 confirmed and five unconfirmed air victories, and his awards by this time included the Gold Bravery Medal for Officers.

After World War 1 Fiala returned to the Technical University in Vienna, where he gained a degree in manufacturing processes, while maintaining his active interest in aviation. In 1925 he became the personal assistant of Professor Hugo Junkers at the Junkers company at Dessau in Germany, where he stayed, in a number of capacities, for the next eight years. He established an airline in Fürth, was head of the Junkers workshops of the Polska Linja Lotnicza Aerolot in Warsaw, in

One of the fighters flown successfully by Linke-Crawford was the Hansa-Brandenburg D I (or KD). This example here is 65.54 *(Bruce Robertson)*

1928–29 he was in Japan to set up that country's first all-metal aircraft manufacturing facility at Mitsubishi, in 1929 he negotiated for Junkers in the USA, and by 1933 had become chief engineer for the entire Junkers company.

After the Nazis took power in Germany in 1933, Fiala was arrested and deported from Germany, but back in Austria continued his work in aviation-related fields: in 1935, for example, he and Julius Arigi established the Wiener-Neustadt Airport Management Association. During World War 2, after Austria's 1938 annexation by Germany, Fiala was a Hauptmann in the German air force, serving as commander of the base at Horsching Linz. He died on 29 October 1964, and in 1967 the Austrian air force base at Aigen in Ennstal was named 'Fiala-Fernbrugg'.

Frank Linke-Crawford, ranked fourth on the list of Austro-Hungarian aces, was born on 18 August 1893 at Krakau, and was the son of Major Adalbert Linke and his English-born wife, Lucy Crawford. In 1910, Linke-Crawford entered the military academy at Wiener-Neustadt, and in 1913 graduated as a Leutnant before being posted to Dragoon Regiment Nr 6. At the outbreak of World War 1 he was in the 1st Eskadron (troop) of this cavalry regiment, which served on the Eastern Front, and in November 1914 was appointed commander of the regimental Infanterie Eskadron (infantry troop). Between October 1914 and October 1915 Linke-Crawford continued to rise in his regiment and received several decorations, but was hospitalised on several occasions with dysentery and malaria.

Linke-Crawford, commanding officer of *Flik 60J* at Feltre, is captured by the camera in front of the Phönix D I of Oberleutnant Jansky (centre) and Aviatik D I fighters *(Bruce Robertson)*

Karl Kaszala could still manage a smile after a disastrous landing at Sesana airfield in May 1917 in a Hansa-Brandenburg KD (D I 28.11). In was in this aeroplane that Kaszala scored his fifth victory

Linke-Crawford then requested a transfer to the LFT, and his request was approved in December 1915. As an officer, he was considered only for observer training, as 'chauffeuring' aircraft was considered a task for non-commissioned officers, and attended the observer school at Wiener-Neustadt. In March 1916, he was posted to the new *Flik 22* unit under the command of Hauptmann Losoncsy. In September 1916, after completing many operational flights as an observer, he received permission to train as a pilot (the role of the pilot had become more properly appreciated in the LFT). After the completion of his training, in January 1917 he was posted to *Flik 12* as Chefpilot (chief pilot and, as such, deputy commanding officer to Hauptmann Arpad Gruber). *Flik 12* was based on the Isonzo front in north-eastern Italy, and here Linke-Crawford became an operational pilot. At first he flew mainly reconnaissance and bombing sorties in two-seat aircraft as well as escort and attack sorties in single-seat machines. He soon gained a reputation for aggressive and determined flying: on a long-range reconnaissance mission over the Tagliamento river, for example, his Hansa-Brandenburg C I (229.08) two-seater came under attack for some 30 minutes by an Italian SPAD fighter. Linke-Crawford completed the mission, however, and returned with 68 bullet holes in his aeroplane. On 2 August, flying solo on an escort mission in an Aviatik C I (37.08), he was shot down (probably by Tenente Colonnello Pier Ruggiero Piccio – 24 victories) but was not injured.

Linke-Crawford poses in front of a Hansa-Brandenburg D I (65.54) of *Flik 12*. This aeroplane was crashed on 7 November 1916 by Oberst Uzelac, commander of the Austro-Hungarian army air service (*Bruce Robertson*)

On 4 August, he was reassigned to *Flik 41J*, a fighter squadron commanded by Hauptmann Godwin Brumowski, located at Sesana some 8 km (5 miles) east of Trieste, flying the Hansa-Brandenburg D I and Albatros D III single-seat fighters. Linke-Crawford gained his first victory on 21 August, shooting down a Nieuport over Monte Santo in Hansa-Brandenburg D I (28.40). Thereafter his score increased quickly and impressively: he despatched his fifth victim on 23 September when he shot down an Italian seaplane at Grado while flying Albatros D III (153.04). Linke-Crawford's first 'double' (his eighth and ninth 'kills') followed on 5 November while he was flying Albatros D III (153.11). He downed a Macchi L-3 flying boat of the Italian *259ᵃ Squadriglia* that crashed on land and then another seaplane that came down in the sea near the Adriatic coast. There followed a second 'double' (10th and 11th 'kills') on 23 November when, flying Albatros D III (153/11), Linke-Crawford shot down a pair of single-seat aircraft in the region of Cortelazzo and Casca di Finanza.

Serving with *Flik 60J* at Feltre during the early summer of 1918, Frank Linke-Crawford is here seen in the cockpit of the Phönix D II (122.01) powered by a 149 kW (200 hp) Hiero inline engine *(Bruce Robertson)*

Soon after achieving his 13th victory, Linke-Crawford was appointed to the command of a new unit, *Flik 60J*, late in December. This unit was based near Grigno in the Val Sugana, some 100 km (60 miles) north-north-west of Venice, in an airfield located in a basin inside mountains rising to a height of 1525 m (5,000 ft) that was swampy and prone to partial flooding. *Flik 60J* flew Phönix D I fighters of the 128, 228 and 328 series, and the operational area for its seven pilots was the northern end of the Piave front against a growing Allied air strength dominated by the British but with Italian and French aircraft also involved. From this new base, Linke-Crawford added six more victories to his tally, these including a 'double' on 10 January 1918 when, in Phönix D I (228.16), he disposed of a Nieuport and a 'Sopwith two-seater'.

In March, *Flik 60J* was relocated to the much better airfield at Feltre, some 25 km (15.5 miles) east of Grigno, and toward the end of the same month received new equipment in the form of the Aviatik D I of the 115 series to supplement its Phönix D I aircraft, which were themselves complemented by Phönix D II and D IIa fighters of the 122 and 422 series respectively. The Aviatik D I was more agile than the Phönix D I, but also considerably less structurally robust. In the middle of the month Linke-Crawford reported that he had grounded all his unit's surviving Phönix D I fighters as a result of the type's tendency to wing trailing-edge failures.

On 10 May, Linke-Crawford scored his first victories (another 'double' as his 20th and 21st 'kills') in an Aviatik D I. In the morning, flying 115.32, he shot down a Bristol F.2B two-seat fighter in flames near Levico, and later in the day drove down a Sopwith Camel. (It is worth noting that Austro-Hungarian pilots seemed incapable of differentiating the Camel flown by the British and the Hanriot HD.1 flown by the Italians, and called both types Camel.) Linke-Crawford's 27th and final victory came on 29 July when in 115.32 he shot down a British two-seater in flames near Valstagna.

Very evident in this photograph of the Lohner-built Aviatik D I fighter (115.20), flown by *Flik 60J* when Linke-Crawford was the unit's commanding officer, is the lozenge type of camouflage. The D I was notorious for its tendency toward structural failure in the air *(Bruce Robertson)*

Josef Kiss was killed after achieving 19 confirmed victories in the air, and had the unique distinction of being awarded posthumous promotion from non-commissioned to commissioned rank
(Bruce Robertson)

The details of Linke-Crawford's final flight are still the subject of controversy. It is known, however, that, again flying 115.32, he became separated from his three compatriots in an engagement with three Camel fighters and then fell in with two Italian HD.1 fighters. Linke-Crawford's Aviatik D I was then seen to spin down (suggesting a wing failure) before recovering and being attacked by one of the HD.1 fighters and coming apart in the air. Linke-Crawford was apparently the sole aerial success of Caporale Aldo Astolfi.

The fifth ranking Austro-Hungarian ace, Josef Kiss, was killed on 24 May 1918, and within 24 hours of his death was posthumously promoted from Offizierstellvertreter to Leutnant in der Reserve, the only Austro-Hungarian pilot to be elevated from non-commissioned to commissioned rank. Kiss was born on 26 January 1896 in Pozsony (now Bratislava). His parents were of humble Hungarian origin, and his father worked as a gardener at the military cadet school in Pozsony. On the outbreak of World War 1 Kiss left school and enlisted despite the fact that his lack of a school matriculation certificate precluded, by the regulations of the Austro-Hungarian army, his much-desired attainment of commissioned rank. On 26 October 1914 the freshly trained Kiss joined the Infanterieregiment Nr 72 on the Carpathian (southern) sector of the Eastern Front. While recovering from a serious wound, he was granted permission to train as a pilot, a task that he undertook at Parndorf and Wiener-Neustadt.

By the end of April 1916 Kiss had joined *Flik 24*, newly created under the command of Hauptmann Gustav Studeny to provide support for the 11th Army. *Flik 24* was located at Pergine in the Val Sugana, on the southern part of the Tyrol front about 15 km (10 miles) east of Trent. Kiss quickly revealed himself to be an able pilot in reconnaissance and fighter missions, and achieved his first aerial victory on 20 June while at the controls of Hansa-Brandenburg C I (61.23) with Oberleutnant Georg Kenzian as his rear-seater. On this occasion Kiss attacked a Farman two-seat reconnaissance aircraft behind the Italian positions on Monte Cimone and forced it down. On 25 August Kiss was piloting a Hansa-Brandenburg C I (26.29), with Leutnant Kurt Fiedler as the observer, when he attacked a Caproni three-engined bomber. The C I took more than 70 hits from the defensive fire of the Italian bomber's guns, but Kiss

Austro-Hungarian personnel, including Josef Kiss at right, are seen with the wreckage of the first Caproni bomber brought down by Kiss, an event that took place on 25 August 1916 *(Bruce Robertson)*

nonetheless forced the bomber down and it crash-landed near Pergine airfield. A third victory followed on 17 September when he forced down another Caproni bomber while flying a Hansa-Brandenburg two-seat biplane with Oberleutnant Karl Keizar as his observer.

It was some nine months before Kiss recorded his fourth victory. By this time his aggression and skill had been recognised and he was usually assigned a Hansa-Brandenburg D I single-seat fighter as his mount.

This Hansa-Brandenburg D I (28.37), flown by Kiss, was one of the few examples of this 'star-strutter' fighter fitted with a synchronised Schwarzlose machine gun in the upper part of the forward fuselage rather than the original armament of one unsynchronised machine gun in a fairing above the upper-wing centre section. Another feature of this aeroplane was the low-aspect-ratio fixed fin added to the upper fuselage ahead of the rudder for improved directional control
(Bruce Robertson)

Flying 28.37 on 10 June 1917, Kiss shot down a Nieuport fighter near Asiago. He racked up his fifth aerial victory only four days later when, in 28.37, he forced down a SAML two-seat reconnaissance aeroplane of the *113ª Squadriglia* near Roana. Flying the same aeroplane on 13 July, Kiss forced down a Savoia-Pomilio two-seater. On 11 September he achieved his final victory while serving with *Flik 24*, in this instance a SAML two-seater that he shot down near Asiago.

During November, Kiss was posted to the *Flik 55J* fighter squadron, which was also based at Pergine. *Flik 55J*'s commander was Hauptmann Josef von Maier, who allocated Kiss as the third member of a flight with von Maier himself and Julius Arigi. Kiss was soon fully integrated into this elite flight and was able to add 12 more victories to his total between the middle of November 1917 and late January 1918. He achieved eight of these victories in company with von Maier and/or Arigi, including a Caproni bomber forced to land and another Caproni shot down in flames (eighth and ninth victories) on 15 November while flying the Albatros D III (153.17), a SAML two-seater on 17 November while flying the Albatros D III (153.47), a pair of Italian aircraft over Monte Summano on 18 November while flying 153.47, another pair of Italian aircraft near Asiago on 7 December in an Albatros D III, and a SAML two-seater on 16 December again while flying an Albatros. Other 'kills' scored by Kiss included a Royal Aircraft Factory R.E.8 two-seater of the RFC's No. 42 Squadron, forced to land at Pergine airfield, a victory shared with Oberleutnant Georg Kenzian and Zugsführer Alexander Kasza. On 26 January 1918, in the Albatros D III (153.47), Kiss achieved his 19th and last victory, a SAML two-seater of the *115ª Squadriglia* that crashed behind the Italian lines. This made Kiss the highest-scoring Hungarian ace of the LFT.

When, on 27 January, the Austro-Hungarians spotted a single enemy fighter over Pergine airfield, Kiss lifted off to intercept but was soon involved in a fight with three aircraft. Both his machine guns then jammed, and the leader of the opposing flight

This SP.2, brought down by Kiss on the Austro-Hungarian side of the lines in July 1917 while he was flying the Hansa-Brandenburg D I (28.37), was so little damaged that it was then taken into Austro-Hungarian service as 00.47
(Bruce Robertson)

Seen in front of the Oeffag-built Albatros D III (153 series) with a pair of British officers, in Sam Browne belts, after these two men's R.E.8 aeroplane had been forced down behind the Austro-Hungarian lines, these Austro-Hungarian pilots include the nine-victory Oberleutnant Georg Kenzian (between the British officers) and Josef Kiss immediately to the right of the right-hand British officer (*Bruce Robertson*)

managed to wound him in the abdomen after Kiss had flown magnificently for some 10 minutes to avoid the Italian pilot's fire. Kiss managed to break off and land at Pergine. It was long thought that Kiss's opponent was the second-ranking Italian ace, Tenente Silvio Scaroni (26 victories), but it now seems more probable that he was in fact Captain M. B. Frew of No. 45 Squadron, RFC.

After a recuperation that was patently too short, Kiss returned to service. On 24 May, still very weak, Kiss lifted off in Phönix D IIa (422.10) with two other pilots and became involved in a large dogfight. Far below his best, Kiss was shot down and killed by a British fighter, probably flown by 2nd Lieutenant G. A. Birks of the RAF's No. 66 Squadron.

With 18 confirmed victories, and one unconfirmed, Franz Gräser ranks sixth on the list of Austro-Hungarian aces although he never completed any formal pilot training course and therefore never received his pilot's certificate. Gräser was born on 18 October 1892 at Nyir-Mada in Hungary and, on the outbreak of World War 1, was a student at the technical university in Budapest. In October 1914 he joined the Infanterieregiment Nr 72 and, following the completion of his training, attended the reserve officer school at Esztergom until the middle of July 1915. He was then posted to the Eastern Front where, between August 1915 and July 1916 with the exception of five weeks in hospital as a result of wounds, he commanded a machine gun detachment.

During the late summer of 1916 Gräser volunteered for the LFT and was posted to the school at Wiener-Neustadt where officers were trained as observers. On 1 August he was gazetted as a Leutnant in der Reserve, and at the end of October was posted to *Flik 2*, commanded by Rittmeister Eugen Graf Somssich de Saard, on the Isonzo front in northeastern Italy. It soon became evident that Gräser's capabilities were in the field of air photography and aerial gunnery. On 10 February 1917 he scored his first victory. He was the observer in a Hansa-Brandenburg C I two-seater flown by a non-commissioned officer. His aeroplane tackled a Farman two-seater of the Italian air service and forced it to crash-land in the vicinity of Jeza, to the west of Tolmein. However, Gräser's aeroplane was so badly damaged that it too had to make a crash-landing.

In May Gräser was posted to another unit on the Isonzo front, *Flik 32* commanded by Hauptmann Richard Hubner. It was with this unit that

Seen in typical smiling pose in front of a Hansa-Brandenburg C I two-seater of *Flik 32* in the summer of 1917, Franz Gräser finished sixth on the list of Austro-Hungarian aces with 18 confirmed and one unconfirmed victories

Gräser achieved his second victory when, on 20 May, in a Hansa-Brandenburg C I, he and Feldwebel Franz Wognar, his pilot, forced down an Italian SPAD over Monte Sabotino. Gräser then began to learn to fly, largely under the tutelage of another of *Flik 32*'s pilots, Feldwebel Franz Fraueneder. From September 1917 he started to fly on reconnaissance missions as the pilot rather than as the observer.

At the beginning of October Gräser was posted to *Flik 42J* based at Prosecco just to the north of Trieste, and commanded by Hauptmann Ladislaus Hary. The unit's primary equipment was the Albatros D III, the type Gräser flew for the rest of his career. He began his time with *Flik 42J* with four victories in the first three days of the Battle of Caporetto. One victory on 25 October was followed by a 'double' on the following day when he shot up and exploded an Italian observation balloon before, later in the day, intercepting and shooting down near Lake Doberdo an Italian fighter attempting to tackle the aircraft he was escorting to and from the naval air station at Trieste. This Nieuport was Gräser's fifth victory.

On 23 November Gräser shot down an Italian seaplane in flames near Agenzia close to the mouth of the Piave river. This was his first victory in the Albatros D III (153.44) that was to become his best-known mount with an owl painted on each side of the fuselage. On 29 November Gräser claimed his tenth victim when he forced down a SAML two-seater.

The following January, Gräser was posted to *Flik 61J*, a new fighter squadron located at Motta di Livensa under the command of

This Phönix-built Hansa-Brandenburg D I fighter (28.47), the first with the low-aspect-ratio fin added to improve directional stability, was flown by Hauptmann Karl Nikitsch, a minor ace who amassed a total of six victories *(Bruce Robertson)*

Oberleutnant in der Reserve Ernst Strohschneider, who was already a double ace in his own right. Gräser and Strohschneider worked together to claim *Flik 61J*'s first victory, a seaplane forced down in the lagoon of Palude Maggiore on 26 January. On 24 February, Gräser was one of several *Flik 61J* pilots involved in shooting down a Macchi M-5 flying boat. On 8 March, flying Albatros D III (153.106), he destroyed an observation balloon above a platform anchored in the Cenesa channel. On 12 March, once again in 153.106, Gräser brought an Ansaldo SVA-5 single-seat reconnaissance aeroplane down in flames near Monastier di Treviso as his 16th 'kill'. On the same day he shot down another SVA-5, but no confirmation was possible. On 16 March, again in Albatros D III (153.106), he collaborated with Strohschneider in bringing down an SVA-5 near Casonetti. On 23 March, in Albatros D III (153.111), Gräser increased his tally to 18 by sending a SAML two-seater down in flames near Noventa di Piave. This was Gräser's final victory.

On 17 May, in response to a request by *Flik 12P* for a fighter to escort one of its reconnaissance aircraft, Gräser lifted off in Albatros D III (153.221). The two Austro-Hungarian aircraft were intercepted over Treviso by Italian fighters, and Sergente Antonio Chiri in a Hanriot HD.1 (supported by two other pilots in similar fighters) shot down Gräser in flames.

Credited with 16 confirmed victories, and one unconfirmed, Eugen Bönsch is ranked seventh on the list of Austro-Hungarian aces. He was born on 1 May 1897 to ethnic German parents in Gross-Aupa, a village of the Sudeten region of northern Bohemia. After completing a course on mechanics and machine manufacturing at a trade school, he volunteered for the Austro-Hungarian army in 1915 and, after completing his basic training, received permission to transfer into the LFT. Bönsch was initially posted to *Fliegerersatzkompanie 6* as a mechanic, but in 1917 was accepted for flying training, completed at *Flek 8* on 22 June. He was promoted to corporal six days later, and in August was posted to a new fighter unit, *Flik 51J* located at Haidenschaft on the Isonzo front in the north-eastern part of Italy under the command of Rittmeister Wedige von Froreich and, later, Oberleutnant Benno Fiala. Destined to become one of the LFT's premier fighter units, *Flik 51J* was equipped with the Albatros D III, initially in its 53.2 and 153 series and later in its 253 series with a more powerful engine.

Bönsch gained his first victory on 1 September 1917 when, in 53.57, he shot down a Nieuport fighter over Monte San Gabriele. The next 'kill' followed in the evening of 28 September when Bönsch, in 153.35, evaded

The type favoured by Eugen Bönsch for his 'balloon busting' missions was the Albatros D III, seen here in the form of 53.21, an Oeffag-built machine manufactured shortly before Bönsch's favourite 53.57 *(Bruce Robertson)*

the attentions of two defending fighters and the fire of ground-based guns to destroy an observation balloon to the north of Plava. On the following day he downed a Nieuport fighter to the south of the same town.

It was 1918 before Bönsch scored again. On 21 February, flying 153.35, he sent an RFC Sopwith Camel down in flames in the area south of Papadopoli (an island in the middle of the Piave river). This was his fifth victory. On 10 March he led a flight of three *Flik 51J* fighters to intercept a force of Caproni bombers, escorted by seven HD.1 fighters, involved in a raid on the airfields at San Martino and Portobuffole. The three Austro-Hungarian pilots flew with such determination and aggression that the bombers jettisoned their bomb loads and turned for home. On the following day Bönsch was part of the escort for Austro-Hungarian bombers attacking the airfield at Marcon. He swooped down to low level and so effectively demoralised the Italian gun defences with his strafing attacks that the bombers were able to go about their work with minimal interference. Later in the day Bönsch was escorting a reconnaissance aeroplane and fought off a succession of attacks by three Camel fighters.

On 12 March Bönsch and other *Flik 51J* pilots undertook a low-level dawn attack on Marcon airfield with bombs and machine gun fire. *Flik 51J* repeated this type of operation on the airfield at Treviso on 16 March, and on the harbour of Portegrandi on 18 March.

Bönsch returned to 'balloon busting' on 3 April when, in 153.140, he brought a balloon down in flames to the south-west of San Biaggio. The ground war was notably intense along the Piave section of the front at this time, and during the early part of April he flew many ground-attack missions, the most important targets being artillery batteries. However, on 17 April Bönsch showed that he had not lost his touch in air combat by engaging and bringing down, a SAML reconnaissance aeroplane near Monte Grappa. On 3 May he shot down another observation balloon, to the north-west of Monastier di Treviso, but the victory was unconfirmed. On 16 June he scored a confirmed observation balloon near Breda di Piave while flying 153.140.

The Battle of the Piave required intensive ground-attack work by the LFT, and 20 June was a notably intense day for Bönsch, who flew several low-level bombing and strafing attacks as well as downing a single-seat reconnaissance aeroplane over the Montello as his tenth confirmed victory. On 8 August, while flying 253.37, Bönsch attacked and ignited an Italian observation balloon.

In the climactic Battle of Vittorio Veneto from 24 October, Austro-Hungarian air strength had reached an abysmally low level (one report spoke of only 29 serviceable aircraft available to the Army of the Isonzo), but Bönsch was one of the pilots who made his presence felt in these few aircraft. On 27 October he disposed of a Camel and an R.E.8, on the following day an HD. 1, and on the day following that another HD. 1 as his 16th and last confirmed victory. Bönsch was also shot down during this time. He escaped from his blazing aeroplane by parachute and, evading capture, returned to his comrades.

After the war Bönsch became an innkeeper, but in World War 2 was called into German service with the rank of Hauptmann to command the airfield at Oschatz in Saxony. After World War 2 he returned to civilian life and died on 24 July 1951.

Ranked eighth on the list of Austro-Hungarian aces, Stefan Fejes was a pilot as much at home in two-seaters as single-seaters as shown by his tally of six victories in the former and 14 in the latter. Fejes was born on 30 August 1891 in the town of Raab in Hungary. He was conscripted into the Hungarian 14th Infantry Regiment in 1912, and on the outbreak of World War 1 was still in uniform. After being severely wounded in September 1914, he was in hospital for almost six months and in March 1915 was posted to the army's motor service. Then, in May 1916, Fejes was approved for pilot training, which he completed early in 1917 before being posted as a Zugsführer, in February of that year, to *Flik 19*. This unit was based at Haidenschaft on the Isonzo front in the north-eastern part of Italy under the excellent command of Hauptmann Adolf Heyrowsky. *Flik 19* flew an assortment of aircraft types including various types of two-seater including the Hansa-Brandenburg C I in several of its series.

Fejes achieved his first victory on 17 April 1917, while on his third operational flight. Flying a Hansa-Brandenburg C I with Oberleutnant Oskar Zeisberger as his observer, he outmanoeuvred a Nieuport fighter that span out of control into the ground outside Görz. On 14 May Fejes downed another Nieuport near Merna and, six days later, downed a SPAD near Britof to the south of Görz.

On 19 June the Hansa-Brandenburg C I manned by Fejes and Leutnant in der Reserve Josef Purer was flying in the region of Sober (now Vertojba) when it was seen by a flight of Nieuport fighters, which swept in to the attack. Fejes was determined to make a fight of it as his aeroplane had two fixed forward-firing machine guns in the so-called 'baby coffin' container above the upper wing and a trainable machine gun in the rear cockpit, and so turned toward the attackers. The Austro-Hungarians downed two of the Nieuport fighters (only one of which was confirmed), but their own machine was so badly damaged that Fejes had to make an emergency landing near Schonpass.

On 26 July both Fejes and his observer for the day, Leutnant Alexander Tahy, became aces. During the eight months he spent at *Flik 19*, Fejes achieved six victories, but these were ancillary to this intrepid pilot's main tasks, which were the humdrum roles of all two-seaters of the time, notably bombing, reconnaissance and artillery observation.

During October 1917 Fejes was posted to an elite unit, *Flik 51J*, which had been the third dedicated fighter squadron to come into LFT service when it was established at Haidenschaft in July 1917 under the command

A pilot who is probably Stefan Fejes is depicted in the cockpit of an Oeffag-built Albatros D III fighter (53.24) *(Bruce Robertson)*

of Rittmeister Wedige von Froreich. After the Battle of Caporetto, *Flik 51J* was relocated to Ghirano airfield some 50 km (31 miles) to the north-north-east of Venice. *Flik 51J* remained at Ghirano until near the end of World War 1 and, including in its strength a large number of capable pilots, was notably well equipped with Albatros D III single-seat fighters.

On 3 December 1917 Fejes achieved his first success with *Flik 51J*, sending a balloon down in flames over Visnadello. He next scored on 18 March 1918 when, flying 153.132, he shot down a Camel near Piavon to the west of Salgareda. On 22 March Fejes achieved his tenth victory when he downed an R.E.8 near Susegana-Salleto. On 30 March he became embroiled in a dogfight with an altogether more formidable opponent, the pilot of a Camel who put 46 bullets into the D III (including one round that injured the Fejes' heel) before succumbing to Fejes's fire.

On 3 May, flying 153.140, Fejes shot down a French two-seater near Arcade and then, later in the day while flying 153.155, shot down an Italian observation balloon to the north-west of Monastier di Treviso. Neither of these victories was confirmed, however. Fejes reached a total of 15 victories on 15 June 1918 as the Battle of the Piave began, when he brought down an Italian SPAD fighter. The last victory confirmed to Fejes followed on 1 September when, in 253.54, he shot down a Camel near Arcade, for his 16th victory. Another victory achieved over Candelu 11 days later remained unconfirmed. Thus the final tally for Fejes was 16 confirmed and four unconfirmed victories.

At the end of the war when the Austro-Hungarian Empire was dissolved, Fejes returned to Hungary, now under communist rule. When Hungary was invaded by Czechoslovak, Romanian, and Serb forces in 1919, Fejes enlisted in the Red Air Corps which was helping to defend Hungary and was on the strength of the 8th Squadron, this formation's only fighter unit. He was forced down in May 1919 as a result of damage to the propeller of his Fokker D VII fighter, and remained a prisoner of the Czechoslovaks until the end of fighting later in 1919.

Thereafter Fejes was an instructor in the clandestine Hungarian air force (created in defiance of the terms of the Treaty of Trianon that had ended Hungary's war with the Allies) from 1928, an airline pilot between 1930 and 1940, and in World War 2 a transport pilot with the Hungarian air force. Thereafter Fejes fades from recorded history.

Ranking ninth overall on the list of Austro-Hungarian aces, Ernst Strohschneider was born on 6 September 1886 in Aussig an der Elbe to affluent parents of German ethnic origin. Early details of Strohschneider's career are no longer known, although it is thought that he was an infantryman before the start of World War 1 and was promoted Leutnant in der Reserve in January 1913. At the outbreak of war in 1914 Strohschneider was on the strength of the Infanterieregiment Nr 28, which was deployed to the Serb front, but after recovery from a leg wound was posted to the Infanterieregiment Nr 42 on the Carpathian (southern) sector of the

Caught by the camera in 1917 when he was on the strength of *Flik 19*, Oberleutnant Alexander von Tahy claimed eight confirmed victories before his death on 8 March 1918. The medal is the Silver Bravery Medal, 1st Class, for Officers *(Bruce Robertson)*

This Phönix-built Hansa-Brandenburg C I (129.35) was powered by a 149 kW (200 hp) Hiero inline engine and sported non-standard camouflage. The aeroplane was released to *Flep 1* in April 1917 before being passed to *FIG 1* (later *Flik 101G*) and then, during 1918, to *Flik 21D* and finally *Flik 23D* *(Bruce Robertson)*

Oberleutnant in der Reserve Ernst Strohschneider claimed an eventual 15 confirmed and one unconfirmed victories, and is here captured by the camera at the time he had 12 victories. The ribbon is that of the Military Merit Cross, 3rd Class, with War Decoration *(Bruce Robertson)*

Zugsführer Ferdinand Udvardy claimed eight confirmed victories in the air, and is here seen in the rank of Korporal during 1916 *(Bruce Robertson)*

Eastern Front. Hospitalised by another leg wound in February 1915, Strohschneider later returned to the same regiment as the commander of a machine gun detachment. In September 1915 he was again wounded and this time also captured by the Russians, but escaped and managed to return to the Austro-Hungarian lines. When he had recovered from this third wound Strohschneider was declared unfit for front-line service, but then volunteered for service with the LFT. He trained as an observer at Wiener-Neustadt, and on the completion of this course in March 1916 was posted to the new *Flik 23*, located on the Tyrol front in Italy under the command of Hauptmann Heinrich Kostrba. Strohschneider soon began to make a name for himself with deep reconnaissance flights and bombing attacks on targets such as Treviso and Vicenza, which were well protected by anti-aircraft guns. On 15 June he gained his first aerial victory when he sent down an Italian seaplane in the Sarca valley. He was in a Lloyd C III flown by Oberleutnant Franz Schorn. The victory was unconfirmed, however.

When the campaign on the Tyrol front became less intense, Strohschneider was posted to *Flik 28* on the altogether more active Isonzo front. After only a short time with *Flik 28* he was accepted for flying training. While training as a pilot he also instructed in the observer role. When qualified, Strohschneider joined *Fluggeschwader 1* (later *Flik 101G*), located at Divacco in the north-eastern part of Italy, as the Chefpilot (deputy commander) under Hauptmann Karl Sabeditsch. Strohschneider generally flew the Hansa-Brandenburg D I in the escort role for the unit's bombers, but was not the type of pilot to make the best use of this fighter, and indeed had even crashed in one. Even so, he did achieve his first two confirmed victories during June 1917.

Two months later Strohschneider became the Chefpilot of *Flik 42J* located at Prosecco airfield on the Isonzo front under the command of Hauptmann Ladislaus Hary. His first victory with *Flik 42J* was a 'double' on 23 September. With Zugsführer Ferdinand Udvardy, he drove down a Savoia-Pomilio two-seat reconnaissance aeroplane and a SPAD single-seat fighter, both of which crashed near Kostanjevica. On 26 September Strohschneider claimed his fifth victory in the form of a SPAD fighter. On 25 October, Strohschneider and another of *Flik 42J*'s 'stars', Franz Gräser, scored the first of several 'kills' they claimed together while flying Albatros D III single-seat fighters. The two Austro-Hungarian pilots sent an Italian seaplane down in flames near Grado, and on 15 November Strohschneider, again in company with Gräser, achieved his tenth victory when he short down a fighter near Monastier di Treviso.

On 28 December Strohschneider became the first reserve officer to be given command of an LFT squadron when he was appointed to lead *Flik 61J*, newly created as a pure fighter unit at Motta di Livensa on the Piave front some 40 km (25 miles) to the north-east of Venice. The airfield was also home to another new fighter squadron, *Flik 63J*, and when this unit's designated commander, Hauptmann Karl Nikitsch, was injured in a crash, Strohschneider was asked to lead both squadrons as tactical commander. Strohschneider was joined in *Flik 61J* by his friend Gräser, and the two men picked up where they had left off with *Flik 42J* with a shared victory on 26 January 1918 over a seaplane, which fell near Lagune Palude Maggiore. In the same month Strohschneider expressed his unhappiness with the Aviatik D I fighter saying that the type's control system 'was obviously designed by someone who had never flown'. Strohschneider gained his 15th and final victory on 16 March when, in an Albatros D III (153.119) and accompanied by Gräser, he shot down an SVA-5 that crashed near Casonetti to the west of Cavazuccherina.

During the night of 20/21 March Strohschneider led a flight of five aircraft in a night bombing attack on the Italian positions near Zenson, but crashed while landing in Phönix D I (228.36) and was killed.

With 12 confirmed victories, Adolf Heyrowsky was ranked tenth on the list of Austro-Hungarian aces, but was also one of the most important tactical air leaders produced by the Austro-Hungarian Empire. He fought right through World War 1, and was a front-line airman for almost three years without any significant break in a career that spanned a large number of aircraft types and a considerable diversity of roles. His victory tally was creditable in itself, but was made remarkable by the fact that 11 of the 12 victories were amassed while Heyrowsky was flying two-seat aircraft (he was Austria-Hungary's leading two-seater ace), and were therefore incidental to the tasks that were Heyrowsky's primary responsibility. This success was not achieved without loss, however, for Heyrowsky was shot down three times and wounded at least twice.

The son of a gamekeeper, Heyrowsky was born on 18 February 1882 in the Styrian town of Murau. He graduated from the Infantry Military Academy in Prague in 1902 and began his army career as an Offizierstellvertreter on the strength of Infanterieregiment Nr 9, being promoted to Leutnant in May 1904 and then Oberleutnant in May 1910. In 1912 Heyrowsky volunteered for the Austro-Hungarian army's aviation arm, qualifying as a pilot in August of that year. On the outbreak of World War 1 he was posted to *Flik 2*, operating over the Serb front, as a pilot. *Flik 2* had to deal with a determined enemy as well as desperately poor conditions and obsolete aircraft, the latter comprising six Lohner Pfeilflieger biplanes that had not been flown since December 1913. Heyrowsky immediately started to make a name for himself with numerous reconnaissance flights often as deep as 200 km (125 miles) behind the Serbian front line and, on one occasion at least, an attack on a Serb pontoon bridge with bombs whose external fuses had to be lit by hand before release.

In November 1914 Heyrowsky became commander of the new *Flik 9*, also located on the Serb front. On 22 February 1915 he achieved his first aerial victory when, in a two-seater, he attacked and shot down an observation balloon near Belgrade. Ten days later he shot down another balloon in the same area. His success as a tactical air leader and pilot was recognised by his promotion, out of seniority, to the rank of Hauptmann.

In August 1915 Heyrowsky became commander of the new *Flik 12*, based behind the Isonzo front in the north-eastern part of Italy, and remained with this unit until the beginning of 1916, when he became commander of the new *Flik 19* at Haidenschaft, also behind the Isonzo front. Under Heyrowsky's excellent leadership, *Flik 19* emerged as the

Feldwebel (later Offizierstellvertreter) Friedrich Hefty of *Flik 12* scored five confirmed and four unconfirmed victories to reach 36th on the list of Austro-Hungarian aces

The design by Ernst Heinkel is strongly evident in the deep rear fuselage, high-set tailplane and rudder of this Phönix-built Hansa-Brandenburg C I two-seater of *Flik 12*. The photograph was taken in June 1918 *(Bruce Robertson)*

As well as being an ace in his own right, Adolf Heyrowsky was an important figure in the development of the Austro-Hungarian army air service's general operational capability. Here he is depicted with, from left to right, the Order of the Iron Cross, 3rd Class, with War Decoration and Swords; the Military Medal Cross, 3rd Class, with War Decoration and Swords; the Silver Military Merit Medal; the Bronze Military Merit Medal; and the Karl Troop Cross *(Bruce Robertson)*

The Phönix D IV (20.24) was a potentially excellent fighter that reached only the prototype stage. It was demonstrated at the July 1918 evaluation of new Austro-Hungarian fighters at Aspern with an advanced reflector gun sight *(Bruce Robertson)*

best of all the Austro-Hungarian two-seater squadrons, and one that at various times had on its muster a number of celebrated airmen including the aces Benno Fiala, Stefan Fejes, Franz Rudorfer, Alexander von Tahy, Ludwig Hautzmayer and Josef Purer, as well as a number of other first-class pilots and observers. *Flik 19*'s equipment comprised a wide assortment of Albatros and Hansa-Brandenburg two-seaters and, on occasion, single-seat fighters. Heyrowsky's favourite aeroplane was the Hansa-Brandenburg C I (29.64), on which he achieved five of his victories.

It was on 4 May 1916 that Heyrowsky achieved his third victory when, with Oberleutnant in der Reserve Benno Fiala as his observer in the Hansa-Brandenburg C I (61.55), he attacked the Italian airship M 4 over Merna. Heyrowsky and Fiala had armed one of their aeroplane's machine guns with explosive rounds designed to puncture lighter-than-air craft and then ignite the resultant mix of inflammable hydrogen and air. The Italian ship burst into flames and crashed to the ground.

In a pair of decidedly odd episodes during the 5th and 6th Battles of the Isonzo, Heyrowsky volunteered for service as an infantry officer when he was not flying, and served as commander 16th Field Company of the Infanterieregiment Nr 27. He played a notable part in the 6th Battle of the Isonzo, troops under his command being largely responsible for preventing an Italian breakthrough at San Michele. He also flew during this battle, logging many flights, six of which resulted in combat. During this time Heyrowsky scored two more victories and was also shot down twice. On 9 August 1916, while flying the Hansa-Brandenburg C I (61.61), he was attacked by nine Italian aircraft (one Voisin, five Caudrons and three Nieuports) and after a 45-minute battle was forced down behind the Austro-Hungarian lines as his own aeroplane was damaged. It was repaired during the night, and on the following day Heyrowsky took off on a bombing sortie. Over Görz the C I came under attack from three Italian aircraft (one Voisin and two Nieuports). After shooting down the Voisin near Cormons, Heyrowsky found that his own aircraft was so badly damaged that it was virtually impossible to control, but managed to effect a forced landing on the Austro-Hungarian airfield at Aisovizza. It was just five days later that Heyrowsky became an ace, as while at the controls of a Fokker A III single-seat fighter (03.42) he brought down a Voisin.

Heyrowsky was involved in seven air combats during the 10th Battle of the Isonzo, and gained another two victories. On 15 May 1917, in Hansa-Brandenburg C I (29.64) with Oberleutnant Ladislaus Mauser as his observer, he managed to shoot down a SPAD single-seat fighter near Merna, and on 3 June, with the same aeroplane and observer, forced down a Nieuport fighter that crashed near Sober as his tenth confirmed victory.

Heyrowsky's last two victories were a 'double' on 26 June 1917, when in his favourite C I he shot down a Nieuport and a Caudron over Sober. In October, after being shot down again and avoiding

capture, Heyrowsky was switched away from flying duties to become the Stabsoffizier der Luftstreitkräfte (staff officer for aviation) for the 2nd Army and then, in March 1918, the LFT's liaison officer with Generalleutnant Ernst Wilhelm von Hoeppner, the general commanding the German army air service. While serving with the Germans, Heyrowsky managed to fly on several bombing missions, one of them against the port of Dover in south-east England, and also on a

number of reconnaissance missions. Heyrowsky was an Oberst in the Luftwaffe during World War 2, and died in 1945 just before his promotion to Generalmajor. During World War 2 Heyrowsky recorded his impressions of the Hansa-Brandenburg D I, which he considered a wholly indifferent fighter that was obsolete even as it entered service. The type's ceiling was too low, and its very poor handling characteristics meant that the type was all too prone to enter a sudden spin 'with consequent casualties'.

Kurt Gruber, the son of a teacher, was born in 1896 in Linz. He was ranked 11th on the list of Austro-Hungarian air aces and was one of the LFT's most popular figures. Much of Gruber's formal education was completed in Sachsen-Altenburg, Germany, where he studied to be an engineer. However, on the outbreak of World War 1 Gruber was called into service with the Austro-Hungarian army and later volunteered for the LFT. His application was accepted and, as a result of his training in technical matters, he was trained as a pilot.

Gruber's initial operational posting arrived in August 1915, when he was allocated to *Flik 1* on the Eastern Front. Under the command of the redoubtable Hauptmann Otto Jindra, *Flik 1* was a general-purpose unit and, in common with most other units on the Eastern Front at this time, operated mainly in the reconnaissance and artillery spotting roles with an assortment of two-seat aircraft types. Gruber began to make a name for himself as an excellent pilot, and soon virtually every observer/gunner officer in the unit was enthusiastic about the prospect of flying with him. In September 1915 Gruber was promoted to Zugsführer, and in January of the following year was awarded an important decoration, the Silver Bravery Medal, 1st Class.

On 14 April 1916 Gruber opened his victory tally when, with Hauptmann Egon Hervay von Kirchberg as his observer/gunner in a Knoller-built Albatros B I (22.30), he tackled a Russian army air service Morane-Saulnier parasol monoplane and shot it down into no-man's-land near Bojan. Some 18 days later Gruber achieved his

Placed 11th on the list of Austro-Hungarian aces, Offizierstellvertreter Kurt Gruber achieved 11 confirmed victories over the Eastern and Italian Fronts *(Bruce Robertson)*

second victory when, on 2 May in B I (22.30) with Oberleutnant Godwin Brumowski as his observer/gunner, he encountered another Morane-Saulnier parasol monoplane. Both Gruber and Brumowski fired at the Russian aeroplane, but it was Gruber's fire that was credited with sending the Russian aeroplane down behind the Russian lines.

Some five weeks later, in achieving his third victory, Gruber made a small mark in aviation history with the first 'kill' by an Austro-Hungarian pilot on the Eastern Front without the support of an observer/gunner. On this occasion, 6 June, Gruber was flying the two-seat B I (22.30) as a single-seater and by skilful use of his machine gun, forced a Morane-Saulnier parasol monoplane to make a forced landing behind the Russian lines at Dolcok. This earned him a rare second award of the Silver Bravery Medal, 1st Class, and Gruber also received the highest award of the Austro-Hungarian Empire for a non-commissioned officer, the Gold Bravery Medal. On 1 June he was promoted, well before the appointed time based on seniority, to Feldwebel (sergeant major) and then only some 10 weeks later, on 11 August, to Stabsfeldwebel (staff sergeant).

In the middle of December 1916, Gruber was transferred to the Flieger Arsenal where, for five months, he was involved in the testing and evaluating of new aircraft. One of the aircraft on which he reported was the Hansa-Brandenburg C II, which he said was easy to fly and lacked the vices of the same company's D I, but was nonetheless lacking in climb rate, directional stability and pilot's fields of vision. It was only in the middle of May 1917 that Gruber was posted back to the front, this time to the LFT's first genuine fighter squadron, *Flik 41J* based at Sesana on the Isonzo front in the north-east of Italy. The unit's commanding officer was Hauptmann Godwin Brumowski, who had once been an observer/gunner in the rear seat of a two-seater flown by Gruber on the Eastern Front. *Flik 41J* was equipped with the Hansa-Brandenburg D I (or KD) fighter. This type possessed tricky handling characteristics, and the fact that Gruber had not yet fully mastered the type was shown on 21 May when, in D I (28.14), he span into the ground from low altitude over the airfield at Sesana. Gruber survived the resulting crash, but did not return to operational duty until late September of the same year.

The enforced lay-off obviously spurred Gruber, and by the time he was posted away from *Flik 41J* during December 1917 he had been awarded a second Gold Bravery Medal in recognition of the dash and success with which he had flown. On 29 September, almost certainly while at the controls of an Albatros D III, Gruber encountered an Italian army air service Nieuport fighter and rapidly disposed of his opponent, which fell behind the Italian lines at Cormons. Just 10 days later Gruber became an ace as he set fire to an Italian observation balloon near Isola Morosini just after the crew had taken to their parachutes.

Gruber was posted to *Flik 60J* on 23 December 1917. This new squadron was created at the notably small, mountain-girt and easily flooded airfield located near Grigno, some 95 km (60 miles) to the north-west of Venice in the Val Sugana, and was under the command of Oberleutnant Frank Linke-Crawford, who had served with Gruber in *Flik 41J*. The new unit was equipped with one of the best Austro-Hungarian fighters, the Phönix D I, a type that was not notably agile but more than compensated for this fact it its structural strength and ability to absorb combat damage. Each of *Flik 60J*'s aircraft was painted with a white band round the fuselage behind the cockpit, and on this band was painted the first letter of the usual pilot's name. In D I (228.24) 'G', Gruber scored five victories.

The new unit opened its account on 10 January 1918 when Linke-Crawford and Gruber ran into a flight of Allied fighters over Valstagna. In the following dogfight, the two pilots disposed of two of the Allied fighters in victories credited as Linke-Crawford's 14th and 15th and Gruber's 7th and 8th 'kills'. On 27 January, Gruber tangled with a fighter he described as being a Sopwith single-seater but which was probably in fact a Hanriot HD.1 and, at the end of a long dogfight, shot down the Italian fighter over Valstagna. On 1 February he brought down a Nieuport fighter near Vattaro to the south of Col Moschin as his ninth confirmed 'kill', and some 25 days later notched up his 10th victory when he intercepted another Italian 'Sopwith' (and again probably an HD.1), shooting it down near Monte Nuova.

Gruber is seen in the cockpit of his Oeffag-built Albatros D III fighter of *Flik 41J* at Sesana airfield on 5 October 1917

In the first part of 1918 Gruber was awarded the Gold Bravery Medal for the third time, becoming one of only six LFT non-commissioned officers to receive such an accolade. On 1 April Gruber was promoted to Offizier-stellvertreter (deputy officer), the highest non-commissioned rank in the Austro-Hungarian army. This occurred only three days before Gruber's death on 4 April. After taking off in his favourite D I in company with three other *Flik 60J* aircraft, Gruber and his comrades arrived in the area over Primolano but were 'bounced' by two flights of Sopwiths. Gruber disposed of one of the Allied fighters, but almost immediately afterward his fighter was hit by a long burst of machine gun fire and its wing cellule collapsed. The resulting crash was inevitably fatal, and Gruber was buried with full honours in the military cemetery at Feltre two days later. The posthumous award of a fourth Gold Bravery Medal was one of two such awards made, Julius Arigi being the only other person to receive four Gold Bravery Medals.

Ranking 12th on the Austro-Hungarian list of aces with 11 confirmed and two unconfirmed victories, Franz Rudorfer was born on 29 July 1897 in Vienna, and on the outbreak of World War 1 volunteered for service in the army. Emerging from his basic training at the Reserve Officers School, he was posted to the Infanterieregiment Nr 59 and was promoted to Leutnant in der Reserve in August 1916. In May 1917 Rudorfer requested a transfer to the LFT and was trained as an observer at Wiener-Neustadt before being allocated to *Flik 19* under the command of Hauptmann Adolf Heyrowsky on the Isonzo front in north-eastern Italy.

Rudorfer soon made a name for himself as a first-class observer who excelled in the reconnaissance and artillery observation aspects of his role. He was credited with his first victory on 15 November 1917 when the two-seater in which he was the observer behind Zugsführer Josef Schantl shot down an observation balloon to the north-west of Carbonera. While with *Flik 19* Rudorfer started learning to fly, and in April 1918 he was

posted as a single-seat fighter pilot to *Flik 51J* based, like *Flik 19*, at Ghirano and equipped with Albatros D IIIs of the 153 and later the 253 series.

It was on 17 April that Rudorfer opened his account with *Flik 51J*, bringing down a SAML two-seater over Monte Grappa in the D III (153.141), which became his favourite aeroplane and the machine in which he scored five confirmed and one unconfirmed victories. In this aircraft Rudorfer scored a 'double' on 1 May. In company with three other *Flik 51J* pilots, Rudorfer fell in with a force of seven Camel fighters near Bocca Callalta. The pilots of *Flik 51J* immediately attacked, and in the tangled dogfight that followed Rudorfer shot down one of the Camel fighters in the region of Cimadolmo. In the same fighter but later in the day, Rudorfer shot down an Italian observation balloon in flames near San Biaggio.

Rudorfer was again flying the same D III when he became an ace on 6 June, shooting a SPAD fighter down in the region of Salettuol and Roncadelle. Another victory on the same day, in this instance a Camel, was not confirmed for lack of third-party witnesses and poor visibility. The same factors were responsible for Rudorfer's other unconfirmed victory, a two-seater shot down on 11 September. In the same month Rudorfer became commander of *Flik 51J* when Benno Fiala left the unit.

Flying against very heavy odds in the Battle of Vittorio Veneto, the campaign that decided Austria-Hungary's defeat in World War 1, Rudorfer was one of the few Austro-Hungarian pilots who was able to get airborne. On 24 October, flying D III (253.124), he shot down an observation balloon in flames at Breda di Piave, and three days later closed his account with a pair of Camel fighters downed over the Island of Papadopoli. Although he survived World War 1 and was belatedly awarded his pilot's certificate in December 1918, Rudorfer died of unknown causes on 13 November 1919.

Placed 13th on the list of Austro-Hungarian aces with a tally of ten confirmed victories, Friedrich Navratil fought as a front-line soldier and airman throughout World War 1, his only 'breaks' being the period when he trained as a pilot, and bouts of recuperation from four major wounds. Navratil was born to Croatian parents on 19 July 1893 in Sarajevo. After finishing school, he decided on an army career and, on graduation from the Infantry Cadet School Libenau, joined the Bosnian-Herzegovinian Infanterieregiment Nr 1, in which he was a Leutnant on the outbreak of World War 1. The regiment fought initially on the Serb front, and Navratil was wounded in August and December 1914 before the regiment was transferred to the Italian front. Navratil's prowess was recognised in July 1915 by 'out-of-seniority' promotion to Oberleutnant.

Although of poor quality, this photograph of *Flik 51J* personnel at Ghirano in the summer of 1918 includes four of Austria-Hungary's most important aces: in the wicker seat is Benno Fiala, the unit's commanding officer, with Oberleutnant Franz Rudorfer (11 confirmed and two unconfirmed victories) seated to his right. Behind Fiala's left elbow is Stefan Fejes, with Eugen Bönsch standing immediately to the right of him

Franz Rudorfer poses in front of his favourite fighter, the Oeffag-built Albatros D III (153.141) of *Flik 51J* at Ghirano in the summer of 1918

The regiment was later involved on the Montenegrin and Romanian fronts between periods on the Italian front, and Navratil was again wounded in December 1916. In January 1917 Navratil volunteered for the LFT, and on the completion of his training at Wiener-Neustadt as an observer, was posted in July 1917 to *Flik 13*, a unit located in Galicia on the Eastern Front. Navratil's service in this theatre was not particularly distinguished, and in October of the same year he was transferred to *Flik 11*, another unit in the Galician region, but completed only two flights with this unit before the effective end of operations in this theatre.

Oberleutnant Friedrich Navratil is caught by the camera in the cockpit of the Oeffag-built Albatros D III (253.116) at Romagnano airfield, home of *Flik 3J* in the summer of 1918

Navratil then asked for pilot training, starting his course in November 1917 and being posted to the advanced flying school at Campoformido in northern Italy during January 1918. He was earmarked for a fighter unit, and in March 1918 reached *Flik 41J* based at Portobuffole under the command of Hauptmann Godwin Brumowski and flying the 153 series of the Albatros D III.

Navratil in fact scored only one victory with *Flik 41J*. On 17 April and while escorting a two-seater in the D III (153.157) accompanied by Brumowski in another D III, he tackled a force of seven aircraft that tried to intercept the two-seater. The two Austro-Hungarian pilots drove off the Allied fighters, which lost a single Camel that was credited as Navratil's first and Brumowski's 31st victory.

On 9 June Navratil became commander of *Flik 3J* which was located at Romagnano in the south Tyrol, about 8 km (5 miles) south of Trent and equipped with the Albatros D III in its 153 and later its 253 series. His first victory with *Flik 3J* came on 28 June when, flying the D III (153.198), he shot down one of three Italian SPAD fighters in the region of Zugna-Ospedaletto. On 16 July, with Navratil flying the D III (253.06) in company with the fighters flown by fellow *Flik 3J* pilots Oberleutnant in der Reserve Stefan Stec, Oberleutnant Franz Peter and Stabsfeldwebel Otto Forster, the four Austro-Hungarian fighters fell in with an equal number of HD.1 fighters from the Italian *72ª Squadriglia* and disposed of three (one shot down and the other two forced down). Navratil was credited with two of these victories as his third and fourth 'kills'. One week later, Navratil became an ace when, operating in the area of Monte Pasubio and the Val di Chiese, he encountered two F.2B Fighters of the British No. 139 Squadron; he drove off one and shot down the other.

In the rest of August 1918 Navratil notched up another five victories in the D III (253.06). On 5 August, came an SIA.7B two-seater of the *121ª Squadriglia* near Romagnano. Then, on 10 August, Navratil met an SVA-5 single-seat reconnaissance biplane escorted by two single-seat fighters. Navratil's attack dispersed the Italian aircraft, allowing the Austro-Hungarian pilot to close on and down one of the fighters that crashed into a ravine near Monte Pasubio. Next, on 16 August, Navratil intercepted four of No. 139 Squadron's F.2B Fighters and shot down one of these aircraft, that crashed in flames near Trent. On 23 August, another of No. 139 Squadron's F.2B Fighters fell to Navratil, whose fire into the aeroplane's engine and fuel tank forced its pilot to make an emergency landing on the Austro-Hungarian airfield at Gardolo. Lastly, on 31 August, Navratil and Stec led four inexperienced pilots over the front line. The Austro-Hungarian force spotted an F.2B Fighter and attacked it, Navratil downing the machine as his tenth victory, but in the meantime the inexperienced pilots had been 'bounced' by Camel fighters of No. 45 Squadron, RAF, and were all shot down, three of the pilots being killed and the fourth wounded and taken prisoner.

Navratil blamed himself for the disaster, and during September and October he undertook only one operational sortie. On 21 October he was performing a test flight in the D III (253.06) when his seat broke, and in the following emergency landing he was badly injured. This ended his career in World War 1, but after the war he joined the air force of the newly created Yugoslavia, eventually rising to the rank of general. In April 1941 Germany conquered Yugoslavia and created a puppet state in Croatia. Navratil became the minister of War in this state, but his complaints about the brutality of the regime led to his removal. Even so, he was convicted of war crimes by the communist regime of Yugoslavia after the war and executed in 1946.

Raoul Stojsavljevic was ranked 14th on the list of Austro-Hungarian aces with ten confirmed victories He was born on 28 July 1887 at Innsbruck to an Austrian mother and Croatian father. Stojsavljevic graduated from the Maria Theresa Military Academy in Wiener-Neustadt in August 1908 and received an appointment as a Leutnant with the Feldjägerbataillon Nr 21. In 1913, however, he transferred into the army's air service and in July 1913 qualified as a pilot.

At the beginning of World War 1 Stojsavljevic moved to the eastern Galicia part of the Eastern Front as a member of *Flik 1*. He distinguished himself with this unit, especially for long-range reconnaissance flights, and survived a crash in a Lohner Pfeilflieger biplane (10.14) on 31 July when the aeroplane grazed a chimney while coming in to land and crashed. In November of the same year he was posted to *Flik 13* as the unit's Chefpilot. Forced down by snow on 16 February 1915, Stojsavljevic and his observer set fire to their aeroplane before being captured, but managed

One of the Austro-Hungarian army air service's lesser aces, Feldwebel Johann Riszticz (or Risztics) claimed seven confirmed victories *(Bruce Robertson)*

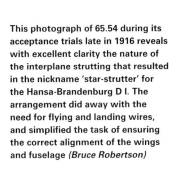

This photograph of 65.54 during its acceptance trials late in 1916 reveals with excellent clarity the nature of the interplane strutting that resulted in the nickname 'star-strutter' for the Hansa-Brandenburg D I. The arrangement did away with the need for flying and landing wires, and simplified the task of ensuring the correct alignment of the wings and fuselage *(Bruce Robertson)*

to escape six days later and hid out in a number of places around and in Lemberg (now Lwow) before it was recaptured by the Austro-Hungarians on 22 June.

Late in the summer of 1915, Stojsavljevic was posted to *Flik 17* on the Tyrol sector of the Italian front, but in September he moved to *Flik 16*, of which he became the commander in December. *Flik 16* was stationed at Villach in south-eastern Austria, and was equipped with two-seaters. Stojsavljevic often teamed with Leutnant in der Reserve Josef Friedrich as his observer, and they became one of the best two-seater crews of World War 1. This two-man team first achieved success in air combat on 4 July 1916 when, flying in the Hansa-Brandenburg C I (64.14) on an artillery observation sortie, their aeroplane was attacked by a pair of Farman two-seaters. The fire of the Austro-Hungarians hit the fuel tank of one of the Italian aircraft, which was forced to land behind the Austro-Hungarian lines. The same two-man team scored two more victories later the same month and in August. On 1 September, Stojsavljevic flew with another observer, and brought down a Farman two-seater in the Val Dogna.

In late 1916 Stojsavljevic asked for permission to train as a single-seat fighter pilot, and in February 1917 was posted for two months to *Flik 34*, which operated the Hansa-Brandenburg D I. On 13 February, in the D I (65.68) Stojsavljevic shot down a Farman two-seater south of Kostanjevica on the Doberdo Plateau. This was the pilot's fifth victory, but Stojsavljevic was not altogether happy in the D I, for he crashed at Zaule while trying to land a fighter of this 'star-strutter' type and suffered a knee injury that was a source of discomfort for the rest of his life. He learnt more about being a fighter pilot when, during May 1917, he was attached to *Jasta 6* of the German army air service on the Cambrai sector of the Western Front.

Back in Italy, on 14 July Stojsavljevic was flying the D I (28.30), which he had adapted for the high-speed reconnaissance role with a camera installed in the fuselage, when he encountered a Farman two-seater and shot it down in flames in the region of Monte Crete and Monte Cullar. On 23 July, again in a D I fighter, he gained his eighth victory by downing another Farman. Stojsavljevic gained his next victory on 7 September when flying a D I once more, in this instance near Monte Skarnitz, he met and shot down a SAML two-seater of the *113ª Squadriglia*. He gained his tenth and last victory on 21 November, when he was flying an Albatros D III and shot down a SAML two-seater near Feltre.

Raoul Stojsavljevic in his Hansa-Brandenburg D I 'star-strutter' fighter (28.30) of *Flik 16* on Villach airfield on 14 August 1917. This far-sighted pilot was a pioneer of high-speed photo-reconnaissance (using a captured Italian camera in a fuselage compartment of his aeroplane), and personalised features of this machine include the large windscreen, and the curved rail allowing him to bring down the rear of the two fixed forward-firing machine guns so that he could clear jams

One of the aircraft flown by Raoul Stojsavljevic was a German type, the Fokker M.18 that was known to the Austro-Hungarians as the B III. The aircraft were serialled from 04.11 to 04.27, and the machine illustrated had lateral control by means of upper-wing ailerons rather than the wing warping used in other machines. 04.11 was delivered to *FIG 1* at the end of January 1917, and was reallocated to the *Flek 6* training unit in the middle of March in the same year *(Bruce Robertson)*

Stojsavljevic's luck ran out on 12 January 1918. Flying a reconnaissance sortie in the Hansa-Brandenburg C I (68.07), he was attacked by several aircraft, and had a very difficult time escaping. His aeroplane was badly damaged, and a bullet had also shattered one of his femurs. Struggling to remain conscious despite his loss of blood, he managed to regain his own lines before crash landing. After a major operation and a heroic struggle to achieve a full recuperation against the expectations of his doctors, Stojsavljevic was able to record a virtually full recovery by October 1918. The war was practically over by then, and he was given command of the officers' flying school at Wiener-Neustadt.

After the end of World War 1, Stojsavljevic opted for Austrian rather than Yugoslav nationality, serving in the para-military Flug-Polizei until 1921. After ventures in transport and film-work flying, as well as an interlude in the army, he was forced to leave military service in 1925 and set about the creation of an airport at Innsbruck and the establishment of high-altitude transport flights. On 2 September 1930, Stojsavljevic crashed in thick fog and was killed.

With nine confirmed and 11 unconfirmed victories Gottfried Freiherr von Banfield was placed 15th overall on the list of Austro-Hungarian aces, but first on the smaller reckoning of Austro-Hungarian naval aces. Von Banfield was born on 6 February 1890 in Castelnuovo to a father who was a career officer in the navy. He was educated at the military secondary school in St Polten and in 1905 entered the naval academy at Fiume (today Rijeka). He graduated in June 1909 and was accepted for naval service with the rank of Seekadett, rising to Fregattenleutnant in May 1912. Just one month later von Banfield reported to the flying school at Wiener-Neustadt, where he gained his pilot's certificate in August of the same year. His next task was the evaluation of the Donnet-Lévêque flying boat in France, and the navy later bought two such 'boats.

In November of the same year von Banfield was posted to the naval air station recently created on the island of Santa Catarina off Pola (now Pula), and then had to qualify as a seaplane pilot. In March 1913 a forced landing resulted in severe damage to his right leg, and only excellent medical care saved his right foot. It was more than a year before he was once more ready for duty. After the assassination of the Archduke Franz Ferdinand, von Banfield hastened back to Pola and was posted to fly the Lohner flying boat E.21 allocated to the pre-dreadnought battleship SMS *Zrinyi* for reconnaissance and spotting purposes. Von Banfield and his 'boat

Delivered on 18 May 1914 as the second Lohner Type E flying boat and wrecked on 31 May 1918 after what was, by the standards of World War 1, an exceptionally long career, E.18 was the 'boat in which von Banfield made his first operational flight of World War 1 from Kumbor *(Bruce Robertson)*

A type flown by von Banfield was the Hansa-Brandenburg CC (otherwise KDW), seen here at Trieste during 1917 in the form of the 'boat serialled A.24 *(Bruce Robertson)*

were shore-based at Kumbor on the outbreak of war, and were used for bombing as well as reconnaissance.

Between November 1914 and Italy's declaration of War in May 1915, von Banfield was stationed at Pola, where he tested new aircraft and trained pilots. He was then responsible for the establishment of a naval air station at Trieste, a mere 29 km (18 miles) from the Italian base at Grado and only 145 km (90 miles) east of Venice, to undertake operations over the now-vital northern part of the Adriatic. In February he became the station's commanding officer, a post he held until the end of hostilities. Trieste in due course became home to a large number of very assorted aircraft types, land-based as well as water-borne.

Von Banfield is depicted in the cockpit of the Oeffag-built Lohner Type H flying boat (A.11) with a 149 kW (200 hp) Hiero engine. This 'boat was delivered to the Austro-Hungarian naval air service on 18 October 1916 and scrapped on 5 October 1918 *(Bruce Robertson)*

Standing in the cockpit of this Lohner Type L flying boat (L.16) is Gottfried von Banfield. Note that the barrel of the Schwarzlose machine gun retains the vestiges of its water-cooling jacket much cut-down to reduce its weight. Note also the starting handle (under von Banfield's left arm) for the engine *(Bruce Robertson)*

Von Banfield flew whenever he could, and the fact that 11 of his victories were unconfirmed reflects the fact that they were often scored in the course of patrols over the sea, where third-party confirmation was difficult to obtain. Von Banfield gained his first victory on 27 June 1915, while flying Lohner Type T (L.47) with Seekadett Heribert Strobl Edler von Ravelsberg as his observer: spotting an Italian observation balloon near the mouth of the Isonzo river, von Banfield closed the range and his observer forced down the balloon with machine gun fire. Von Banfield's other confirmed victories came on 23 June 1916 in the Lohner Type M 'boat (L.16) when he forced a French FBA Type C 'boat to alight; 24 June 1916 in the same 'boat when he forced down an Italian Macchi L.1 'boat; 1 August 1916 in the same 'boat when he forced down a Caproni Ca 1 bomber; 6 August 1916 in the same 'boat when he shot down a Caproni Ca 1 bomber; 15 August 1916 in the same 'boat when he forced a French FBA Type H 'boat to alight; 15 August 1916 in the same 'boat when he shot down another French FBA Type H 'boat; 3 December 1916 in the Hansa-Brandenburg CC (A.12) when he forced down a Caproni Ca 1 bomber; and 31 May 1917 in the Oeffag Type H (A.11) when he shot down an Italian seaplane.

Von Banfield's unconfirmed victories came on 1 September 1915 in the Lohner Type T (L.47) when forced down two Italian flying boats (a Curtiss and a Type L); 17 April 1916 in the Lohner Type M (L.16) when he drove down two Italian seaplanes; 13 September 1916 in an Albatros

Von Banfield's favourite mount was the Lohner Type H flying boat (A.11) built by the naval arsenal at Pola. The naval ace achieved five victories (two of them at night) in this 'boat, which was named 'Blue Wonder' and later painted overall in medium blue *(Bruce Robertson)*

Von Banfield (in flying kit) is caught by the camera while reporting to the commander of the Austro-Hungarian naval base at Trieste, Konteradmiral von Koudelka, after a flight in October 1917
(Bruce Robertson)

(K.150) when he drove down a Nieuport fighter; 13 October 1916 in the Hansa-Brandenburg CC (A.12) when he drove down a Farman two-seater; 31 October 1916 in an Albatros (A.3) when he drove down a Caproni bomber; 4 August 1917 in the Oeffag Type H (A.11) when he forced down a Caproni bomber; 2 September 1917 in the same 'boat when he drove down a seaplane; 21 September 1917 in the same 'boat when he shot down a seaplane; and 23 September 1917 in the same 'boat when he forced down a seaplane.

Von Banfield married after the war, and then worked in the company established by his father-in-law for maritime salvage, dying on 23 September 1986 at Trieste.

Whereas Brumowski, Fiala and Gruber had started their careers on the Eastern Front but then gone on to greater things on the Italian Front, Otto Jindra achieved all his air combat successes on the Eastern Front as the pilot of two-seat aircraft, and in addition to his prowess as a pilot was also an extremely capable leader and administrator. His nine aerial victories place him 16th in the ranking of Austro-Hungarian aces.

Jindra was born on 18 March 1886 in Chlumetz, near Wittingau, in Bohemia, and at an early age decided to join the army. When he graduated from the Artillery Academy in Vienna during 1905, he secured an appointment in the 14th Mountain Artillery Regiment. His early career progressed at the stately and even pace ordained for officers in the years before World War 1, and he was promoted to Oberleutnant in December 1912. With the outbreak of World War 1, Jindra's regiment was posted to the Eastern Front, where he initially served as a battery commander and regimental adjutant. It was in this capacity that he fought in the 1st and 2nd Battles of Lemberg, receiving the Bronze Military Merit Medal. However, Jindra had already decided that he wanted to serve in the LFT. With his application for a transfer approved, he became an observer with *Flik 1* on 10 September 1914, operating over the Eastern Front. Using the type of radio transmitting equipment for whose installation Benno Fiala, another member of the unit, was largely responsible, Jindra soon became an outstanding controller of air-directed artillery fire.

However, on 14 November the Albatros biplane carrying Jindra and his pilot, Leutnant Max Hesse, was shot down near Krolik Woloski by fire from a Russian cavalry unit. Hesse managed to land the Albatros behind

This photograph of Hauptmann Otto Jindra was taken late in 1915

Stabsfeldwebel Andreas Dombrowski is photographed while serving with *Flik 29* in March 1918. With six confirmed victories, Dombrowski was 27th on the list of Austro-Hungarian aces

the Russian lines and, after a quick examination that revealed something in the order of 180 bullet 'wounds', the two young men decided that there was no chance of effecting even temporary repairs. They therefore removed all the valuable items they could carry and set fire to the aeroplane before making off and eventually regaining the Austro-Hungarian side of the front lines.

A key moment in Jindra's life came at the end of January 1915, when *Flik 1*'s commanding officer was taken prisoner. Despite the fact that he was only an observer, Jindra was selected to replace the captured Oberleutnant Josef Smetana. On 13 June Jindra achieved his first two victories in the air. Flying as the observer/gunner in a Knoller-built Albatros B I (22.29) flown by Zugsführer Max Libano, Jindra was attacked by a pair of Russian Morane-Saulnier two-seater parasol monoplanes. Jindra and Libano defended themselves with a Mauser pistol and a carbine, and in the course of repeated attacks by the two Russian aircraft, the Austro-Hungarian airmen's fire gradually began to exact its toll on the airframes of the two Russian machines which force-landed in a wood near Dubowice, south-east of Monasterzyska, behind the Russian lines.

It was 27 August of the same year before Jindra achieved another aerial victory. On this occasion, while undertaking a reconnaissance sortie over Czortków in another Knoller-built Albatros B I (22.06) with Feldwebel Johann Mattl at the controls, Jindra was engaged by two Morane-Saulnier monoplanes. Jindra was a good marksman, and the fire of his weapon drove off one of the attackers and shot down the other, whose pilot was wounded and brought his aeroplane down near Tluste, crashing as he tried to touch down.

During 1915 Jindra received the Military Merit Cross, 3rd Class, with War Decoration and Swords, and the Prussian Iron Cross, 2nd Class. Moreover, on 1 September of that year he was promoted to Hauptmann. Late in the year Jindra began at unit level to learn the art of piloting, and by 11 December was deemed sufficiently proficient to become a Feldpilot, receiving the appropriate badge only nine days later.

Under Jindra's increasingly capable leadership, *Flik 1* really came into its own in 1916 and 1917, establishing its reputation as probably the best all-round air unit serving on the Eastern Front. During this time the unit was operating over the Bukowina, the multi-ethnic region between the Carpathian mountains and the Dniester river that was then part of Austria-Hungary but now straddles the border between Romania and Ukraine. Here *Flik 1*, flying an assortment of different aircraft types, undertook the full gamut of two-seater operations including, in addition

This Knoller-Albatros B I (22.06) was the *Flik 1* aeroplane on which Otto Jindra achieved his third victory on 27 August 1915

to the more orthodox reconnaissance and artillery observation, bombing, interception and, on occasion, ground attack.

As a pilot, Jindra got off to a poor start for, on 5 January 1916 while flying a Hansa-Brandenburg B I (05.34), he came under attack near Rarancze and was himself cut by a Russian bullet while another put a hole in the aeroplane's fuel tank. Jindra was compelled to make a forced landing, but thereafter things began to improve for him. On 29 March, for example, Jindra achieved his first victory as a pilot when, at the controls of a Knoller-built Albatros B I (22.23), he brought down a Morane-Saulnier parasol monoplane over Sokal as his fourth confirmed 'kill'. Just 11 days later Jindra became an ace while, flying the aeroplane in which he had claimed his fourth victim and with Leutnant in der Reserve Vlastimil Fiala as his observer/gunner, he attacked a Russian biplane to the south-east of Kamieniec-Podolski. The Austro-Hungarian pilot and observer/gunner forced down the Russian aeroplane, which crashed as its pilot attempted to put it down.

On 12 April 1916, with Oberleutnant Godwin Brumowski as his observer in a Knoller-built Albatros B I (22.23), Jindra attacked a parade in Chotin as it was being inspected by the Tsar Nikolai II: there was total pandemonium on the ground as seven small bombs landed. The Austro-Hungarian aeroplane was then attacked by four Russian fighters, but the qualities of Jindra's flying and Brumowski's accuracy with the machine gun in the rear cockpit resulted in two of the attackers being shot down. One of the Morane-Saulnier parasol monoplanes came down near Iszkowcy, to the north of Chotin, while the second came down to the west of Chotin and crashed while attempting to land.

It was 26 September 1916 before Jindra could be credited with another victory. On this date, with Oberleutnant Eduard Struckel as the observer/gunner of his Hansa-Brandenburg C I (64.23), Jindra was attacked by a pair of Nieuport fighters over Solka: the two Austro-Hungarian officers fought back with determination, and one of the Russian aircraft was forced down when its pilot was hit in the throat by a machine gun bullet and just managed to land his aeroplane before dying. On 18 December of the same year Jindra achieved his ninth and final confirmed victory. Undertaking a photo-reconnaissance sortie in a Hansa-Brandenburg C I (63.06), Jindra saw a Russian observation balloon near Pozoritta and dived on it, his observer liberally peppering this tempting target with machine gun fire as it was forced down with the observer dead in its basket.

Jindra continued as commander of *Flik 1*, and another eventful day came on 13 September 1917, when he was himself brought down for the third time. His Hansa-Brandenburg C I (67.30) suffered major damage from anti-aircraft fire and he was forced to land in a hurry near Kimpolung, fortunately without suffering an injury. The success of Jindra's leadership of *Flik 1* is attested by the commanding officer's several awards and decorations during this period, these including the Silver Military Merit Medal (twice) and the Order of the Iron Crown, 3rd Class, with War Decoration and Swords.

During January 1918 Jindra was finally reassigned, becoming the commanding officer of *Fliegerersatzkompanie 11* (*Flek 11*), but his role with this replacement unit lasted for only a short time before it was sensibly

Feldwebel Julius Busa scored five confirmed victories to be placed 35th on the Austro-Hungarian aces list, and is photographed while serving with *Fluggeschwader 1* on the Italian Front in January 1917

Zugsführer Karl Urban, photographed in the summer of 1916 while serving on the Eastern Front with *Flik 10,* was 48th on the Austro-Hungarian aces list with five confirmed victories

While serving with *Flik 57Rb*, six-victory ace Andreas Dombrowski was a regular pilot in this Hansa-Brandenburg C I (429.36). Both the pilot and the observer are wearing parachute harnesses

Leutnant (later Oberleutnant) in der Reserve Kurt Nachod, photographed in 1915, achieved five confirmed victories to rank 42nd on the Austro-Hungarian aces list

decided that an officer with Jindra's outstanding capabilities would be better employed in a more important role. He therefore became the commanding officer of *Fliegergruppe G*, a group of five bomber squadrons based on the Italian Front and controlled directly by the headquarters of Feldmarschall von Boroevi's army group. However, before he could take up his new role, Jindra was badly injured in a night flying accident, and this effectively ended the career of this outstanding officer in World War 1. In 1918 he received the Military Merit Cross 3rd Class, with War Decoration and Swords for the second time, and was one of only 18 LFT officers to receive the double honour.

After the end of World War 1 and the dissolution of the Austro-Hungarian Empire, Jindra became a Czechoslovak, and as such was the major force in the creation of a Czechoslovak air arm, to whose command he eventually rose. He died in 1942.

Another 11 men who flew over the Eastern Front became aces, although only seven of these gained all their victories over this Front. These seven men were Offizierstellvertreter Karl Kaszala (eight victories), Oberleutnant in der Reserve Otto Jäger (seven victories), Oberleutnant Roman Schmidt (six victories), and Feldwebel Julius Busa, Oberleutnant in der Reserve Kurt Nachod, Feldwebel Augustin Novak, and Offizierstellvertreter Karl Urban (all five victories). The other four men, gaining some of their victories on other fronts, were Stabsfeldwebel Andreas Dombrowski (six victories) and Offizierstellvertreter Friedrich Hefty, Oberleutnant Karl Patzelt and Oberleutnant Rudolf Szepessy-Sokol von Negyes et Reno (all five victories).

APPENDICES

APPENDIX I

ACES OF THE AUSTRO-HUNGARIAN ARMY AND NAVY AIR ARMS

Position	Name and final rank	Victories (confirmed/unconfirmed)
1	Hauptmann Godwin Brumowski	35/8
2	Offizierstellvertreter Julius Arigi	32
3	Oberleutnant in der Reserve Benno Fiala, Ritter von Fernbrugg	28/5
4	Oberleutnant Frank Linke-Crawford	27/1
5	Leutnant (Post.) Josef Kiss	19
6	Leutnant in der Reserve Franz Gräser	18/1
7	Feldwebel Eugen Bönsch	16/1
8	Stabsfeldwebel Stefan Fejes	16/4
9	Oberleutnant in der Reserve Ernst Strohschneider	15/1
10	Hauptmann Adolf Heyrowsky	12
11	Offizierstellvertreter Kurt Gruber	11
12	Oberleutnant Franz Rudorfer	11/2
13	Oberleutnant Friedrich Navratil	10
14	Hauptmann Raoul Stojsavljevic	10
15	Linienschiffsleutnant Gottfried Freiherr von Banfield	9/11
16	Hauptmann Otto Jindra	9
17	Oberleutnant Georg Kenzian Edler von Kenzianshausen	9
18	Offizierstellvertreter Karl Kaszala	8
19	Hauptmann Heinrich Kostrba	8
20	Oberleutnant Alexander Tahy	8
21	Stabsfeldwebel Ferdinand Udvardy	8
22	Oberleutnant in der Reserve Josef Friedrich	7
23	Oberleutnant in der Reserve Ludwig Hautzmayer	7
24	Oberleutnant in der Reserve Otto Jäger	7
25	Hauptmann Josef von Maier	7
26	Stabsfeldwebel Johann Risztics	7
27	Stabsfeldwebel Andreas Dombrowski	6
28	Hauptmann Johann Frint	6
29	Feldwebel Alexander Kasza	6
30	Hauptmann Karl Nikitsch	6
31	Oberleutnant Franz Peter	6
32	Oberleutnant in der Reserve Josef Pürer	6/1
33	Oberleutnant Roman Schmidt	6
34	Oberleutnant Rudolf Weber	6
35	Feldwebel Julius Busa	5
36	Offizierstellvertreter Friedrich Hefty	5/4
37	Offizierstellvertreter Julius Kowalczik	5
38	Feldwebel Franz Lahner	5
39	Fregattenleutnant Friedrich Lang	5
40	Stabsfeldwebel Johann Lasi	5
41	Oberleutnant in der Reserve Bela Macourek	5
42	Oberleutnant in der Reserve Kurt Nachod	5
43	Feldwebel Augustin Novak	5/1
44	Oberleutnant Karl Patzelt	5
45	Leutnant in der Reserve Alois Rodlauer	5
46	Oberleutnant Rudolf Szepessy-Sokol von Negyes et Reno	5
47	Feldwebel Karl Teichmann	5
48	Offizierstellvertreter Karl Urban	5
49	Offizierstellvertreter Franz Wognar	5

COLOUR PLATES

1

Lohner Type C C.11 flown by Offizierstellvertreter Julius Arigi at *Flik 6,* Igalo airfield, Dalmatia, summer 1915

The Lohner Type C (service designation B II) was a two-seat reconnaissance and general purpose aircraft that entered service early in the war. While the front and upper part of the fuselage and the vertical tail surfaces of Arigi's aeroplane were completed in grey, the sides of the fuselage, the horizontal tail surfaces and the upper and lower wings featured the red/white/red stripes of the Austro-Hungarian national markings, replaced in 1915 by black crosses.

2

Lohner Type T L.47 flown by Linienschiffsleutnant Gottfried Freiherr von Banfield, Trieste naval air station, June 1915

In this two-seat flying boat the pilot and the observer sat side-by-side. Von Banfield achieved his first 'kill' in L.47 on 27 June 1915 when he and his observer Heribert Strobl put an Italian observation balloon out of action near the mouth of the Isonzo river. On 1 September the pair had an unconfirmed victory in the same machine, when they forced down a Curtiss-type flying boat east of Grado. The natural finish of doped fabric and wood carried the national markings, the white serial number, the red/white/red national stripes above the upper wing, and the badged red of the tail unit.

3

Oeffag-built Lohner Type H A.11 flown by Linien-schiffsleutnant Gottfried Freiherr von Banfield, Trieste naval air station, 1916–18

Von Banfield achieved his 9th and final confirmed victory in A.11 on 31 May 1917 when he shot down an Italian flying boat at 10.30 p.m. The 'boat crash-landed near the mouth of the Primero river and was towed back to Grado by Italian motor-boats early the next day. The action was notable as the first ever night victory by an Austro-Hungarian flier. With the exception of the black/white national markings on the wings and hull, the black serial number and the red/white national markings on the fin, von Banfield had the 'boat painted blue overall as he believed that this was the best camouflage for over-water operations, especially at night. It was nicknamed the 'Blue Wonder'.

4

Fokker A III 03.52 flown by Ludwig Hautzmayer at *Flik 19,* Haidenschaft airfield, February 1916

Germany supplied a number of these limited-capability monoplane fighters to the Austro-Hungarians for home defence. With the exception of the white backgrounds to the national markings and the burnished aluminium alloy of the engine cowling and forward fuselage, the aeroplane was finished in a dull green colour. Hautzmayer (not an ace) flew with *Flik 19* from Haidenschaft airfield on the Isonzo front.

5

Fokker M.10e 03.09 flown by Offizierstellvertreter Friedrich Hefty at *Flik 12,* spring 1916

This particular aircraft was flown by Hefty when he was based on the Isonzo front though none of his five confirmed victories was achieved in a Fokker. The Austro-Hungarians acquired two-seat M.10e (service designation B I) aircraft from Germany as general purpose machines. The natural finish was broken only by the black serial number and by the red and white national markings applied above and below the upper wing and elevators, below the lower wing and on each side of the inverted-comma rudder.

6

Phönix-built Hansa-Brandenburg D I (probably KD 28.40) flown by Oberleutnant Frank Linke-Crawford at *Flik 41J,* Sesana airfield, spring 1917

Fourth in the ranking of Austro-Hungarian aces with 27 confirmed victories, Linke-Crawford served on both the Eastern and the Italian fronts. Having managed to get into Godwin Brumowski's elite *Flik 41,* Linke-Crawford achieved his early victories in KD 28.40 before transferring to the Albatros D III. The red/white chequer was his personal marking. Phönix had originally been Albatros's Austro-Hungarian subsidiary, a fact reflected in the use of the Albatros logo on the balance portion of the rudder.

7

Hansa-Brandenburg D I (probably 28.11) flown by Offizierstellvertreter Karl Kaszala at *Flik 41J,* Sesana airfield, May 1917

Kaszala, who fought on both the Eastern and the Italian Fronts, downed a French SPAD two-seater in KD 28.11 on 20 May 1917 near Monte Santo on the Italian Front. The natural finish of doped fabric, wood and burnished aluminium alloy of 28.11 was broken only by the black of the national markings and the black/white 'ying and yang' personal marking (not necessarily that of Kaszala) on the side of the fuselage.

8

Phönix-built Hansa-Brandenburg D I (probably 28.58) flown by Stabsfeldwebel Johann Risztics at *Flik 42J,* Sesana airfield, July 1917

Seven-victory ace Risztics flew with *Flik 42J* when it was based at Sesana airfield near Trieste. The natural finish of doped fabric, wood and burnished aluminium alloy of 28.58 was broken only by the black national markings and the black-shadowed white '3' that was a personal marking, not necessarily that of Risztics as the aeroplane was flown by a number of pilots.

9

Oeffag-built Albatros D III 153.06 flown by Hauptmann Godwin Brumowski at *Flik 41J,* Sesana airfield, August 1917

Brumowski was the Austro-Hungarian 'ace of aces' with 35 confirmed and eight unconfirmed victories, scoring his early successes on the Eastern Front before taking command of *Flik 41J* in April 1917. On 19 August flying 153.06 he brought down a Caudron two-seater near Karbinje-Ivangrad for his 15th victory and his first in an Albatros fighter. The natural finish of doped fabric and wood carried the national markings under the lower wing, above the upper wing and on the rudder, and the black/white personal marking on the side of the fuselage.

10

Oeffag-built Albatros D III (probably 153.12) flown by Offizierstellvertreter Karl Kaszala at *Flik 41J,* Sesana airfield, summer 1917

The Austrian aircraft manufacturer Oeffag built the German Albatros D II and D III under licence. Most LFT fighter pilots preferred the Albatros D III to the Aviatik D I, although the latter was built in larger numbers. The aeroplane has a natural finish of doped fabric and wood, with black-painted struts and national markings under the lower wing, dark green paint with ochre swirls on the upper fuselage and tail unit, white-outlined national markings on the upper wing and rudder, and black/white personal marking on the side.

11

Oeffag-built Albatros D III 153.15 flown by Offizierstellvertreter Julius Arigi at *Flik 55J,* Haidenschaft airfield, September 1917

At this stage *Flik 55J* was based at Haidenshaft on the Isonzo front. Arigi achieved his 13th victory in 153.15 when he forced down a SPAD fighter at Merna, S.E. of Gorizia. Arigi, arguably the finest all-round pilot in the LFT, was second (after Brumowski) in the Austro-Hungarian list of aces with 32 confirmed victories. With the exception of the black of the national markings, serial number and Arigi's 'skull and crossbones' personal marking, 153.15 was flown in its natural finish.

12

Oeffag-built Albatros D III 153.11 flown by Oberleutnant Frank Linke-Crawford at *Flik 41J,* Sesana airfield, October 1917

Linke-Crawford achieved five of his 27 confirmed victories in this aircraft between 23 October and 23 November 1917, when based at Sesana airfield. They were, in order: a Savoia-Pomilio two-seater, two Macchi L-3 flying boats and two Nieuport fighters. Fourth among the Austro-Hungarian

aces, Linke-Crawford was still only 24 years old when killed in action on 31 July 1918. The aeroplane's lower surfaces were left in natural finish, while the rest of the airframe was painted in dark green with small swirls of ochre. The serial number is partially obscured by the pilot's personal marking: a falcon outlined in white.

13

Oeffag-built Albatros D III 53.27 flown by Leutnant in der Reserve Franz Gräser at *Flik 42J,* Prosecco airfield, October 1917

Flik 42J was based at Prosecco airfield near Trieste. From his arrival there in October 1917, Gräser would fly only the D III. While the natural doped fabric and wood was maintained for the undersides of the flying surfaces and the lower sides and underside of the fuselage respectively, the upper surfaces of 53.27 were completed in green with swirls of ochre. The three-pointed black/white emblem on the side of the fuselage was Gräser's personal marking. This outstanding ace achieved 18 confirmed victories but was shot down and killed in May 1918.

14

Aviatik D I 38.04 flown by Offizierstellvertreter Friedrich Hefty at *Flik 42J,* Prosecco airfield, October 1917

The Austrian Aviatik D I, designed by Julius von Berg, was built in greater numbers than any other Austro-Hungarian fighter and was the equal of any Italian fighter of the period. Hefty gained just one of his five victories in a D I while flying on the Italian Front. This aircraft was left in natural finish except for the grey painted struts and aluminium alloy cowling, the national markings (including renditions on the wheel covers) in black, and the upper surfaces of the wing and horizontal tail surfaces which were in a mottled pattern of mustard yellow overlaid with green and reddish brown.

15

Oeffag-built Albatros D III 153.42 flown by Stabsfeldwebel Ferdinand Udvardy at *Flik 42J,* Prosecco airfield, October 1917

Udvardy (eight confirmed victories) flew with *Flik 42J,* when this unit was based on the Italian Front. The aeroplane operated in natural finish, comprising doped fabric for the wings, tailplane and elevator, and rudder, wood for the fuselage and fin, and burnished aluminium alloy for the engine cowling and propeller spinner. The black-outlined red heart was Udvardy's personal marking, and the halved red/while wheel cover was the squadron marking.

16

Oeffag-built Albatros D III 153.45 flown by Hauptmann Godwin Brumowski at *Flik 41J,* Torresella airfield, November 1917

Brumowski's first kill in 153.45 was an Italian observation balloon on 9 October 1917. He followed this with a further six in 153.45, although during one encounter with Allied fighters the fuel tank ignited, burning away much of the aeroplane's fabric. The basically all-red colour scheme, inspired by that of Germany's 'ace of aces', Rittmeister Manfred Freiherr von Richthofen, was broken only by white-outlined national markings and the black/white skull, a motif which appeared on fighters flown by Brumowski and his men.

17

Phönix-built Hansa-Brandenburg C I 29.64 flown by Hauptmann Adolf Heyrowsky at *Flik 19*, Ghirano airfield, late 1917

The two-seat Hansa-Brandenburg C I designed by Ernst Heinkel first entered service in 1916. It was later made under licence for the LFT by Austrian aircraft manufacturer Phönix. Heyrowsky gained eight of his 12 victories on the C I, of which four were in this particular aircraft between April and June 1917, when he brought down three Nieuports and a SPAD.

18

Oeffag-built Albatros D III (probably 153.47) flown by Leutnant (Post.) Josef Kiss at *Flik 55J*, Pergine airfield, January 1918

After 112 missions with *Flik 24*, in November 1917 Kiss was transferred to *Flik 55J* based at Pergine airfield north-west of Venice. Kiss achieved four of his 19 confirmed victories in 153.47. The first was a SAML 2-seater shot down in flames on 17 November 1917; his last, and 19th victory, was another SAML on 26 January 1918. An NCO pilot, Kiss was the highest scoring Hungarian ace in the LFT but only achieved officer status after his death in action. With the exception of the black-framed white '7' on the sides of the fuselage, the white-outlined black crosses above the upper wing and on the rudder, the black crosses below the lower wing, and the burnished aluminium alloy of the engine cowling, the aeroplane was completed in blue and blue-green.

19

Oeffag-built Albatros D III 153.46 flown by Feldwebel Eugen Bönsch at *Flik 51J*, Ghirano airfield, February 1918

Bönsch gained all his 12 victories in Oeffag-built Albatros D III fighters between September 1917 and October 1918. In his last combat he was shot down but saved himself by parachute. He landed behind enemy lines but managed to regain his unit. The aeroplane's natural finish was broken by ochre-mottled green details and the national markings. The white-outlined red star on the side of the fuselage was one of several variants of what appears to have been the unit marking.

20

Phönix D I 228.24 flown by Stabsfeldwebel Kurt Gruber at *Flik 60J*, Grigno airfield, February 1918

This was Gruber's favourite aeroplane in which he achieved five of his 11 confirmed victories. It was also the aeroplane in which he was shot down and killed on 4 April 1918 in combat with Sopwith fighters behind enemy lines at Primolano, three days after being promoted to Offizierstellvertreter, the highest NCO rank in the army. This machine was left in natural finish on its lower surfaces, the struts were painted black and the rest of the airframe was painted brown. The fuselage carries the black band indicating the unit and the pilot's initial outlined in white.

21

Oeffag-built Albatros D III (probably 153.106) flown by Leutnant in der Reserve Franz Gräser at *Flik 61J*, Motta di Livensa airfield, March 1918

Gräser achieved five of his 18 confirmed victories in 153.106 while based at Motta di Livensa on the Piave front. The eagle owl was his personal marking. Gräser was shot down and killed while escorting a photo reconnaissance mission over enemy territory on 17 May 1918. Although he received neither formal training nor a pilot's certificate, Gräser ranks sixth on the list of Austro-Hungarian aces.

22

Oeffag-built Albatros D III (probably 153.159) flown by Leutnant (Post.) Josef Kiss at *Flik 55J*, Pergine airfield, April 1918

Kiss scored well during his time with *Flik 55J* at Pergine, adding 12 more victories while flying with von Maier or Arigi. All the lower surfaces and the struts were painted blue, while the rest of the airframe was completed in a mottled scheme of green and brown. The white letter 'K' over a red disk was Kiss's personal marking, and the red/blue triangle represented a medal ribbon.

23

Oeffag-built Albatros D III 153.169 flown by Offizierstellvertreter Friedrich Hefty at *Flik 42J*, Pianzano airfield, June 1918

Hefty achieved three confirmed and three unconfirmed victories in 153.169. Note the red/white of the squadron's wheel covers. Hefty's personal markings appeared as a black-shadowed red '6' and the crowned white letter 'J'; in a white-outlined green oval on the port side, and a red-shadowed black '6' and the crowned white letter 'G' in a similar green oval on the starboard side.

24

Oeffag-built Albatros D III 154.141 flown by Oberleutnant Franz Rudorfer at *Flik 51J*, Ghirano airfield, summer 1918

Rudorfer achieved six victories (five confirmed) in

154.141 between April and June 1918 while flying with the elite fighter unit *Flik 51J* on the Italian Front. His victims included three Sopwith fighters, one SPAD, one Italian SAML and a balloon downed in flames. He achieved ace status on 6 June and ended the war with 11 confirmed victories, although he did not receive his Austrian Pilot's Certificate until three months later. The black/white/yellow/red star on the fuselage of 154.141 was his personal marking.

25
Phönix D I 128.12 flown by Oberleutnant Roman Schmidt at *Flik 30J*, San Pietro in Campo airfield, July 1918
From May 1918 Schmidt flew with *Flik 30J* based on the Italian Front. His first score in 128.12 was on 12 July when he shot down an Italian SAML over enemy territory. He then achieved acedom in 128.12 on 23 July when he shot down a British Bristol F.2B (serial C.4762, 139 Sqn, RAF) over San Godega di Urbano. The pilot and observer were both killed. Schmidt ended the war with six confirmed victories. While the under surfaces of 128.12 were left in natural doped fabric, all other surfaces were painted brown. The red and white motif was *Flik 30J's* unit-selected marking; the blue and white wheel covers were ordained as the unit's marking by the Austro-Hungarian 6th Army.

26
Phönix D IIa 422.30 flown by Feldwebel Karl Teichmann at *Flik 14J*, Feltre airfield, August 1918
Pilots of the elite but doomed *Flik 60J* were dispersed after the deaths of Gruber and Linke-Crawford. Teichman was assigned to *Flik 14J*. Within days he had scored his fifth and final victory in 422.30 when he downed a British Bristol F.2B on 22 August over Monte Asolone. Note the new black and white Balkankreuz on the rudder that replaced the sometimes white-outlined black cross patée used since 1915. The red fuselage band was the unit's marking with the initial letter of the pilot's named outlined in white.

27
Aviatik D I 338.02 flown by Obertleutnant in der Reserve Bela Macourek at *Flik 1J*, Igalo airfield, Dalmatia, August 1918
Hungarian born Macourek achieved his fifth and final victory in 338.02 on 6 September 1918 when he intercepted a British D.H.4 bomber and shot it down in flames into the Adriatic. The under surfaces of 338.02 were left natural, the metal of the struts and cowling was painted grey, and the rest was painted in a lozenge pattern of various greys, browns and greens. The national markings were based on the original type of semi-official 'fat' Balkankreuz. The red/white/green diagonal stripe on the side of the fuselage are the Hungarian national colours – an expression of Macourek's strong feelings for an independent Hungarian state.

28
Hansa-Brandenburg W.18 flown by Linienschiffs-leutnant Gottfried Freiherr von Banfield, Trieste naval air station, August 1918
Von Banfield had been made commanding officer of Trieste naval air station in February 1916, a post he held until war's end. He scored his final confirmed victory in May 1917 but he was involved in many other unconfirmed actions over the sea. This W.18 flying boat was flown by von Banfield during August 1918. Note the crest of Trieste below the cockpit in place of the unit's standard identification numbers.

29
Oeffag-built Albatros D III 253.06 flown by Oberleutnant Friedrich Navratil at *Flik 3J*, Romagnano airfield, August 1918
On 28 June 1918 Croatian born Navratil was appointed CO of *Flik 3J*, a fighter squadron based at Romagnano airfield in the south Tyrol. With only one victory under his belt, he proceeded to score his remaining nine confirmed victories in just over two months, eight of them in 253.06 in a purple period between 16 July and 31 August 1918. The undersides of the flying surfaces of 253.06 were left in their natural finish, the struts and national markings were painted in black, and the rest painted in a mottled dark green pattern. The marking on the side of the fuselage was probably a recognition feature rather than Navratil's personal marking.

30
Oeffag-built Albatros D III 253.04 flown by Oberleutnant Franz Peter at *Flik 3J*, Romagnano airfield, August 1918
Navratil's deputy commander at *Flik 3J*, Peter achieved two of his six confirmed victories in 253.04, the first on 20 August 1918 when he shot down an Italian two-seater behind enemy lines at Vignola and the second on 7 October when he shot down a British Sopwith Camel (E.1498 of No 66 Sqn, RAF) on the road between Trent and Pergine. While the wheel covers and under surfaces of 253.04 were in natural doped fabric, the upper and lateral surfaces were very dark green. The black crosses were not outlined, making them difficult to see. Peter's personal marking was the 'ying and yang' symbol from Chinese philosphy.

31
Oeffag-built Albatros D III 253.116 flown by Oberleutnant Friedrich Navratil at *Flik 3J*, Romagnano airfield, August 1918
Although 253.116 was said to be one of Navratil's favourite fighters, he never scored in this particular aircraft. With the exception of the

natural doped under surfaces, the national markings and serial number, the aeroplane was painted overall in a dark brown/green colour. However, it would be impossible to miss Navratil's personal marking of a large red heart pierced by a long white arrow.

32
Phönix-built Hansa-Brandenburg C I 429.36 flown by Stabsfeldwebel Andreas Dombrowski at *Flik 57Rb,* San Godego di Urbano airfield, autumn 1918
Dombrowski became an ace on the Eastern Front flying various C I two-seaters before being sent to *Flik 68J* on the Italian Front where he notched up his sixth and final victory flying an Albatros D III. He was then assigned to *Flik 57Rb* which specialised in reconnaissance photography, to which he brought skill and experience. The under surfaces of 429.36 were left in natural doped fabric while the rest of the airframe was completed in a camouflage pattern of dark green and tan. The narrow white-outlined black Balkankreuz national markings, replacing the 'fatter' type, appeared as a result of the high command's badly worded original instruction about a change in national markings. The black and white wheel covers were the squadron marking.

33
Nieuport Nie.17 (serial unknown) flown by Captain Aleksandr Kazakov, early 1917
The Russian top scorer in World War I – 20 kills and all scored in Russia – was Aleksandr Kazakov. The Russians relied heavily on French equipment, including the Nie.17. Some were camouflaged in green and brown, but this one retains its French silver finish. Kazakov's unit carried a white skull and crossbones on a black rudder as its marking, but in this case the tail marking is Kazakov's personal black skull and crossbones on a white rudder which allowed his machine to be easily identified.

34
SPAD VII (serial unknown) of Sous-Lt Georges Lachmann, N581, Kamnitz-Padolsk airfield, autumn 1917
The Frenchman Georges Lachmann flew this SPAD from Kamnitz-Padolsk airfield in Russia, as part of the French Aeronautic Mission. In addition to its synchronised Vickers machine gun, he added a Lewis gun on a makeshift overwing mounting and occasionally Le Prieur rockets for balloon-busting missions. Three of Lachman's five successes in Russia were against balloons.

35
Nieuport Nie.11 Ni 1431 flown by Tenente Francesco Baracca, *1ª Squadriglia,* spring 1916
Baracca was the leading Italian air ace in World

War I. He was flying an Nie.11 when he downed his first opponent on 7 April 1916, the first official Italian victory of the war. He went on to fly SPADs. By June 1918 he had scored 34 victories and won his country's top honours before being killed in action on 19 June. This particular machine carried a Lewis gun with an extension to the gun butt.

36
Nieuport Nie.17 (serial unknown) flown by Sergente Cosimo Rizzotto, *77ª Squadriglia,* 1917
Rizzotto's French-built scout was silver-doped overall, whilst the wing V-struts and tail skid were in varnished wood. Without cockades, the fighter nevertheless wore the Italian national colours on its wing undersides – red to port and green to starboard. The *Squadriglia* marking was a red heart painted on the fuselage. The Italian ace was credited with five victories on Nieuports in 1917 and one flying a SPAD in 1918.

INDEX

References to illustrations are shown in **bold**. Plates are shown with page and caption locators in brackets.